CW00848463

Forever Yours

A Sufferer of a Cruel Degenerative Condition Finds Her Voice

Jane Maxwell

WESTBOW
PRESS®
A DIVISION OF THOMAS NELSON
& ZONDERVAN

Copyright © 2018 Jane Maxwell.

All rights reserved. No part of this book may be used or reproduced by any means, graphic, electronic, or mechanical, including photocopying, recording, taping or by any information storage retrieval system without the written permission of the author except in the case of brief quotations embodied in critical articles and reviews.

THE HOLY BIBLE, NEW INTERNATIONAL VERSION®, NIV® Copyright © 1973, 1978, 1984, 2011 by Biblica, Inc.® Used by permission. All rights reserved worldwide.

Scripture taken from the New King James Version®. Copyright © 1982 by Thomas Nelson. Used by permission. All rights reserved.

Scripture taken from the King James Version of the Bible.

This book is a work of non-fiction. Unless otherwise noted, the author and the publisher make no explicit guarantees as to the accuracy of the information contained in this book and in some cases, names of people and places have been altered to protect their privacy.

WestBow Press books may be ordered through booksellers or by contacting:

WestBow Press
A Division of Thomas Nelson & Zondervan
1663 Liberty Drive
Bloomington, IN 47403
www.westbowpress.com
1 (866) 928-1240

Because of the dynamic nature of the Internet, any web addresses or links contained in this book may have changed since publication and may no longer be valid. The views expressed in this work are solely those of the author and do not necessarily reflect the views of the publisher, and the publisher hereby disclaims any responsibility for them.

Any people depicted in stock imagery provided by Thinkstock are models, and such images are being used for illustrative purposes only.
Certain stock imagery © Thinkstock.

ISBN: 978-1-9736-1126-4 (sc)
ISBN: 978-1-9736-1125-7 (hc)
ISBN: 978-1-9736-1127-1 (e)

Library of Congress Control Number: 2017919350

Print information available on the last page.

WestBow Press rev. date: 1/8/2018

FOREWORD

My sister Jane died in May 2016 from a serious degenerative condition called Friedreich's ataxia. Unable to walk and confined to a wheelchair as a teenager, her condition continued to deteriorate over the years. Her ability to speak and be understood was lost relatively early; her sight and hearing went later. Mentally, she remained sharp throughout – as *Forever Yours* will testify – until just before the end, when everything seemed slowly to shut down. Effectively bedridden, she was looked after by a team of dedicated carers. Jane was 60 years old when she died. Her end, when it came, was quiet and peaceful. Hers was a life of unbearable suffering borne with dignity and grace.

Having been effectively silent for many years, Jane's ability to communicate was restored in 2011 through technological advances that enabled her to "speak" via a computer, using very slight movements of her chin. Jane decided to write her memoir. *Forever Yours* is that book – her story, in her own words.

The first part of *Forever Yours*, through to Chapter 20, in which she describes the birth of her son, is Jane's and Jane's alone. From the title of the book to the chapter headings, to the choice of third-person narrative and all the words, this is entirely Jane's creation. Factual errors (and there are more than a few of these) could have been corrected, and footnotes explaining references to unknown people could have been added, but it was thought best to make absolutely no changes at all, leaving Jane's words entirely untouched.

The second part has been created from all the communications that the computer software Jane was using automatically saved. These, too, are all Jane's words, unless expressly indicated otherwise (as in, for example, an on-screen conversation with her husband, Alan). This part of *Forever Yours* has been largely arranged and curated by Alan. The appendices contain other material to which Jane has not contributed, other than the interview with an NHS Trust magazine, providing further information about Jane and filling in some of the gaps in her memoir.

Jane was not able to finish her story as she had intended, as eventually it became impossible to control even her chin and as her mind began to go, so we must rely upon the second part of *Forever Yours* for Jane's thoughts on and observations of the continual slow degradation of all her physical abilities, and many other topics besides. Jane describes the diagnosis of what came to be classified as Friedreich's ataxia in her prologue. Strangely, perhaps, this is not covered in the main text, although it ought to sit halfway through Chapter 13. It is not known whether she intended to add this, perhaps the most difficult part of her story, later or whether it is just others who see it this way. For Jane it may have been just another day.

Friedreich's ataxia is a genetic condition. Recent advances in the field suggest that it is no longer fanciful to believe that one day there may be a cure. Other advances are making the lives of sufferers a little easier with each year that passes. Ataxia UK is the charity that both supports research into Friedreich's ataxia and similar conditions and helps those people with such conditions to lead more normal lives. Please visit their website (www.ataxia.org.uk) for more information.

Finally, we all owe an enormous debt of gratitude to Jane's husband, Alan. His support, care, and love for Jane throughout all her years of gradual decline draws worthy comparison with a saint. *Forever Yours* would have been impossible without him. From his support of Jane in getting her words down to his badgering of the likes of me for contributions, and his expert curating of Jane's apparently random messages, *Forever Yours* stands as a tribute to not only Jane's life of suffering but also the love of a husband.

John Dawe
Ascension Island, March 2017

Smiling baby Jane (Auckland, 1956)

CONTENTS

PART II: JANE'S OTHER WRITINGS

APPENDICES

AUTHOR'S NOTE

Forever Yours is based on my life story as I remember it. I thought it might be encouraging to people with progressive conditions and maybe interesting to others. I would like to dedicate it to my darling, long-suffering husband, Alan, without whom I wouldn't even be here at all. I am very grateful to Helen Day, my speech therapist, who devised a method by which I can write, using assistive technology (the Grid 2).

PART I

A Memoir

Blithe youth is like a smile,
So mirthful, and so brief.

Robert Nicoll

PROLOGUE

*I*t was a cold, wet February evening in 1969. Thirteen-year-old Jane had spent most of the day watching ambulances being unloaded in the courtyard below. She wondered about the people on the stretchers. Had they been in an accident? Or, like her, were they there to undergo tests and for observation?

Although she was on the fifth or sixth floor, Jane occasionally thought she saw a covered stretcher, presumably carrying a dead body. Jane had always had a morbid fear of being buried alive, ever since she'd seen a recent *Sherlock Holmes* episode on TV in which a woman was drugged and placed in a coffin on top of a corpse. Jane also had a morbid curiosity about morgues, and when she put this together with how she enjoyed her dad giving her spoonfuls of blood from the Sunday roast,

Sunday roast – Peter, Jane, and Pam

she amused herself with the thought that she had in fact been a vampire in a previous existence!

Jane's parents had brought her to the hospital about a week before for tests to try to find out why she had become so unsteady. She'd been to see a couple of consultants earlier, and an orthopaedic surgeon had referred her to Great Ormond Street because they thought her problems might be neurological.

Jane enjoyed all the tests, except the EEG (or brain wave test), which involved attaching electrodes all over the head with a most unpleasant sticky substance which messed up her hair.

Originally, Jane had been admitted to a children's neurological ward, but because all the other children were so young, she had been given a private room.

At 13, Jane was already becoming a woman. She was beginning to develop physically. In fact, one of her first periods had arrived during this hospital stay, which was very embarrassing for her. Jane loved reading romantic stories and was starting to dream about becoming an actress (or perhaps a brain surgeon!), and about boys, falling in love, getting married, and having children of her own. All of this made what was to happen next all the more cruel.

It was already dark when Jane's consultant and his registrar came into the room with her parents. She had had no tests for several days as they were working out a diagnosis. The doctors had obviously told her parents about it already. It was not good news. Jane could see that immediately. When the consultant spoke to her, everyone else looked at their feet. "I'm afraid you'll never walk again," he said, "and you may only live for another three years."

Jane was absolutely devastated, and all of her dreams were shattered in a single moment.

CHAPTER 1

Auckland, 1957

"*D*inner's ready, Jane. It's your favourite – sausage and mash!" called Jane's mother. Her mother had been born in New Zealand (though her parents had emigrated from Scotland), while Jane's father (who was a junior doctor at a nearby hospital) had been born in India. His family, who had their roots in Cornwall, had emigrated to New Zealand when he was a boy.

"You can play with Peter after your nap."

Jane, seventeen months old, had been playing with the coal in the coal shed, and as a consequence, she was quite filthy. On hearing her mother's call she came toddling up the side of the small wooden bungalow. She liked playing with Peter almost as much as she loved sausage and mash!

Jane's friend Peter Hillary, who was 3 years old, lived next door to Jane's family in Epsom, Auckland; he was the son of the famous mountaineer Sir Edmund Hillary.

It was a cool late summer's day. Clouds covered the sky, and it looked as though it might rain at any moment. Only the weekend before, Jane's family had gone to the beach with her paternal grandparents. Grampa and Ganygan had joined them because they lived near the beach. Their house was rather posh and old-fashioned, with a stuffed tiger (or was it a rug?) in the front room, which Jane was terrified of. Grampa claimed to have shot it, but everyone knew he hadn't really. Grampa had a very tickly moustache, and Jane would squeal with delight whenever he kissed her. They had had a lovely time splashing around at the water's edge. Only Jane and Grampa had actually got wet. Ganygan preferred to keep an eye on proceedings from her deckchair. Afterwards, they had had dinner; Jane always preferred the pudding or dessert, because Ganygan wasn't very good at cooking meat.

Jane and Grampa on the beach

"Hello, darling," said Jane's mother cheerfully, "this is your new little sister, Mary." Jane looked at the small bundle in her mother's arms and felt a sudden stab of jealousy. Who was this little creature?

"Look what I've got for you!" exclaimed her father. "An old lady I've been looking after made this just for you when she heard Mummy and I were expecting another baby." He held out a rather strange-looking fabric animal with a cloth body and a woolly head.

After Jane had worked out in her head that it was Mummy who had had the baby and not Daddy, she grabbed the animal out of her father's hands. It was love at first sight! "This is Mandy," she said. "This is my new baby!"

"Your little sister has also got you a present," said her mother. "You could take your new 'baby' for rides in it." Her parents produced a small white toy pram made of wicker, which they had originally thought Jane would use for Henry, her beloved first teddy bear (who had previously been her mother's first teddy).

She had pulled all of Henry's fur out while she had been meant to be having a nap, so he looked rather strange, but she loved him anyway. Perhaps this new little sister wasn't that bad after all, although she did wonder how she had managed to get to the shops.

Jane placed Mandy in the new pram and tucked her in, using the new bedding that her mother had thoughtfully provided.

"Aren't you going to thank your sister?" asked her mother.

Jane eyed the small bundle cautiously and, moving closer, looked down at the sleeping baby; she thought that the new baby really was quite nice after all, and that it might be worth including her in the family.

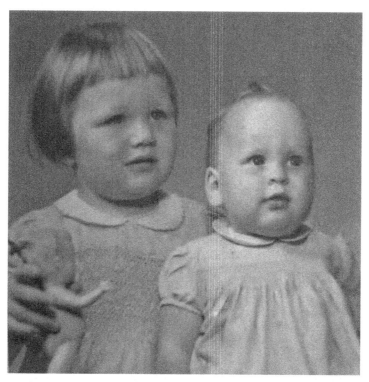

Jane with little sister Mary, 1957

5

While Jane's mother was in the maternity hospital having Mary, Jane had stayed with her maternal grandparents. Nanny was, in her opinion, quite nice, but Grandee was really funny with their cat, Thomas, especially when they shared a bottle of whiskey! Then Thomas would go crazy and start leaping around all over the place. Jane's maternal great-grandfather had once been a millionaire, but unfortunately he had left all of the family wealth to the Salvation Army on account of Grandee (the notorious "Black Dog McGruer"), who had been the black sheep of the family.

Nanny holding Jane at her christening, Auckland, Christmas Day 1955

Jane and Mary with their mother and Grampa
and Ganygan at Mary's christening

As a consequence, Jane's mother had developed, quite understandably, a lifelong aversion to the Salvation Army. When they would come around collecting donations, she could be heard muttering, "You've had more than enough already!"

Jane's family decided to return to the United Kingdom shortly after she'd turned 2. There were more opportunities for doctors to specialise in London. Her father was to be the ship's doctor on a cargo ship. Jane stood holding Grandee's hand and looked up into his face; she asked mournfully, "Will I ever see you or Nanny again … or Thomas?"

Jane with Grandee before leaving New Zealand

Grandee smiled down at his small granddaughter. "I don't know about Thomas, but Nanny and I might visit you in England someday. You never know!"

It was then time to board the ship, so Jane's father led her up the gangplank while her mother followed, carrying Mary. A very lively talkative sailor named Lub led them to their quarters. "These 'ere be yer cabins!" he enthused. "They be right luxurious 'ompared with us, but you be doctors!"

He opened the door to the rather small suite of cabins. Jane turned to her mother and enquired curiously, "Mummy, are you and Daddy doctors?"

Her mother, who was in the process of unpacking, answered hurriedly, "Yes, both Daddy and I have medical qualifications, but I'm not going to work until all my children are older."

Jane was quite alarmed by this. After all, she was just getting used to Mary. How many children did Mummy intend to have?

Just over an hour later, when the unpacking had been completed and Mary had been changed, the family went up on deck to wave goodbye both to Jane's grandparents and to New Zealand, maybe forever.

CHAPTER 2

1958, en voyage

*I*t was a particularly lovely morning in early March. The sun was dancing on the waves all around the ship. Miss Studham, an elderly resident on board, burst open her cabin door and exclaimed, "Oh my goodness, Jane, it's just too hot out here! Don't you have a hat to wear? You're bound to get sunstroke – or worse – if you don't wear one."

Miss Studham was a senior figure in the New Zealand Red Cross. She had taken a shine to Jane. They were kindred spirits, both being rather bossy. One day, Miss Studham commandeered the sailors to make a paddling pool for Jane on the deck. The "pool" (made out of a large crate covered with a tarpaulin) quickly became Jane's pride and joy, and she would spend hours sitting there, imagining she was on a lovely sandy desert-island beach in the shade of palm trees, being served her favourite treats of chocolate cake, scones with cream and jam, roast beef and Yorkshire pudding, and sausages and mash, all on a silver platter like a queen.

Jane wasn't the only one who enjoyed the pool. Miss Studham could often be found sneaking her hot feet into the cool water of the paddling pool, and sometimes Jane's mother would hold a delighted Mary in the water next to her – although Jane could never resist the temptation to splash her baby sister. This would only make Mary cry, and although this would make Jane feel rather guilty for a moment, she reasoned that it was her pool after all.

Jane in her paddling pool en route to England

A few days later, however, Mary did something that made her big sister feel rather proud of her. One minute she was crawling around inside the ship, and the next she was sick all over the cook's head. She achieved this feat by throwing up down a ventilation shaft in the roof of the kitchens, which opened up onto the floor of the passenger deck, where Mary happened to be crawling just after lunch. From that day onward, Jane regarded her little sister with a new kind of respect common to 2-year-olds.

Pam on deck with Jane and Mary, 1958

Next, the ship had to sail through the Panama Canal in order to reach England. Jane's family was allowed off the ship for two hours there to stretch their legs. This was in fact the only opportunity to leave the ship during the six weeks of the voyage. There were docks at the beginning of the canal, and then the scenery became quite beautiful – not that Jane really appreciated its beauty at the time. Everyone else would spend hours on deck, watching the passing views.

Once the ship approached England, the sea became increasingly rough; both Jane and her father suffered from seasickness, which was unpleasant, to say the very least. She hated being unwell, or to be more precise, she hated being sick. She didn't really know why. Perhaps just because of the resulting sour taste in her mouth.

Anyway, Jane hated to have to stay in bed when she could be doing something much more interesting, like playing in the paddling pool when the weather was warm enough, or playing doctors and nurses in Daddy's surgery (or medical room, as it was known on board). Mandy or Henry would be her patients, and they would be tucked up in bed and cured of some dreadful disease.

Jane's father, in contrast, spent much of his time on board pulling teeth for awkward passengers and crew who had developed toothache on the open sea.

One morning, Jane woke up just as the ship was pulling in to Tilbury Docks. She looked out the window. *This must be England!* she thought. *I wonder what it is like and what will happen now. Maybe I will meet the new Queen.*

CHAPTER 3

Ealing, 1958–59

*I*t was a gloriously sunny early May morning when Jane's family found themselves heading towards Ealing, a suburb of London, where her parents' friends lived. They were both doctors who had been there for six months already.

Jane stared out of the taxi window and asked, "Aren't we going to see the Queen?"

Her mother, who was bouncing Mary on her knee, answered, somewhat absent-mindedly, "Not today. We might go up to town soon, though. There are lots of interesting places to see there."

Jane was slightly disappointed to have to wait, as everyone had told her the ship was docking in London.

Ealing was a pleasant leafy suburb with a lovely common. Jane's parents' friends had a little boy, Thomas, whom Jane's mother often minded while his mother was at work. The three children were often put in the bath together. Jane was rather sorry for poor Thomas having to cope with that thing between his legs. She just couldn't imagine doing a wee-wee with it!

After a week or so, the family moved a few streets to their own ground-floor flat with a garden of their own and with a swing for Jane and Mary.

The new flat was so large that the toilet was very difficult to find on the first day. They were worried there might not be one! Eventually it was found down a long corridor, far from the bathroom. The grass in the garden was so long that Jane's father had to use shears before he could tackle it with a lawnmower. Jane was really disappointed when he cut the grass, because she liked to pretend that the garden was a jungle where she was either an intrepid explorer like David Livingstone or a wild lion that would roar fiercely at poor little Mary.

Jane in the garden at Ealing with Mary

There were young children living upstairs. Jane enjoyed playing with them occasionally, and with their farmyard animals. Generally, though, other children in the United Kingdom didn't really seem to be as friendly as the children in New Zealand.

The family's first holiday in England was in East Looe in Cornwall, where Jane's father had relations: his auntie Helen, who was famous for her thinly sliced home-made bread (and who would eventually live to be over 100); her husband, Uncle Roy; their son, John; their daughters, Mary and Ann (the latter of whom was in the United States); and also Auntie Maisie and her elderly husband and extended family.

"Mummy, why is that lady so fat?" enquired Jane, pointing at poor Auntie Helen,

Jane and Mary with their mother, Auntie Helen,
and her daughter, "Auntie" Mary

which was quite amusing, as she herself was more than a little podgy, probably the result of her own overindulgence in her mother's good cooking!

In September, Grandee died and Jane was distraught. She asked her mother plaintively, "Will Grandee go to heaven?"

Her mother replied, with tears in her eyes, "I'm sure he will – and we'll all be together someday."

Jane was rather alarmed by this, because however nice heaven was, she was looking forward to a long, happy life first. And then she remembered Thomas, the cat, and wondered if he had gone to heaven as well to be with Grandee.

Nanny came to stay with the family in early December, just in time for Christmas. Soon after, she started to become very unwell, profoundly depressed. Jane and Mary quite naturally thought she was just sad because Grandee had died, but Jane's parents knew it was more serious than that. Nanny was becoming very confused, so she couldn't really be left alone.

It made sense to send Jane to nursery school, as her mum now had Nanny to look after, in addition to the children.

So, on a lovely sunny April morning, Jane and her mother drove to the private nursery school which was situated in a rather grand old home. She was wearing her new uniform, which made her feel very important. They went into a large room with brilliant sunshine streaming in through the windows. A teacher sat at the head table, with children at a high bench in front of tables to one side of her and toys and games to the other.

Jane in her St Aidan's uniform

"You must be Jane Dawe," boomed the teacher, sounding like a sergeant major. "Sit next to Carol over there," she continued. "She'll show you where to hang your blazer first, and then, after registration, she can show you around."

In no time at all Jane was looking forward to her school day. Just before the family moved to Bexleyheath, to be closer to her father's work, she won a race at their Sports Day and was presented with a prize by none other than Lord Baden-Powell, the son of the founder of the Scout Movement.

Jane receiving her prize from Baden-Powell

When her family first arrived in Ealing, Jane's father attended Hammersmith Postgraduate Medical School. He was then appointed medical registrar at St Nicholas Hospital in Plumstead. The time he spent travelling there from Ealing, however, was terribly gruelling, so the family moved.

Each Christmas morning, Dr Dawe would take the children with him
to carve the turkey for his patients' Christmas lunch. Here he is at St
Nicholas Hospital on Christmas morning, 1958, with Jane and Mary

Just before this, her mother gave birth to a baby boy, Jane's little
brother, John, with the middle name Reed, which was an old family
name, and one especially popular for boys.

Jane thought the baby was lovely, and felt very proud when she was allowed to hold him, as though she were his mother. Mind you, it did seem rather unfair that just because he too had that strange thing between his legs, like Thomas, he should be considered more important than *her*.

Jane, Mary, and baby John enjoying a bedtime story with their father (1960)

CHAPTER 4

Upton Road, 1959–61

he move to Upton Road took place on a rather dismal November morning, which seemed most appropriate to Jane, because she had really liked living in Ealing and didn't want to leave.

The family crammed into their blue Ford Popular stuffed with belongings and set off for their new home in Bexleyheath.

"I do wish Daddy's job wasn't so far away," cried Jane. "Then we could have stayed in Ealing. I don't suppose our new garden will be as big as Ealing Common. Nanny used to love taking us there for walks before she got too sad."

As they approached Central London, the well-known 1950s smog descended over the city and it was impossible to see anything.

Jane's father had to walk in front of the car and lead the way, while her mother got out of the back (leaving John safe in his carrycot, with strict instructions to the two girls to mind their baby brother), moved into the front, and began steering the car.

The house in Upton Road

Eventually, to everyone's relief, they reached their new furnished house in Upton Road, Bexleyheath. It was too dark to see much of the outside, but when they went inside, it seemed like a very old-fashioned sort of house, the kind that perhaps once had servants. Jane had been told stories about such houses before and had found all this fascinating. However, before her imagination ran wild, she found she was just too tired. Her mother led the way to two comfortable beds for her and Mary next to the bedroom she herself was going to share with Jane's father and baby John.

When Jane had had a quick breakfast the next morning, she set off to explore the house more. The house was long and thin, with a large dining room, a small scullery, and a tiny kitchen downstairs. Upstairs there was an enormous front bedroom for Jane's parents, with the girls' large sunny bedroom next to it. Then there was a toilet, a separate bathroom, and at the back of the house, a small bedroom for Nanny, which was rather dark, as trees had overgrown the bedroom windows.

Outside, there was quite a large garden surrounded by trees and, to one side, the "section" which was to provide the perfect location for endless hours of imaginative play, picnics, and fun.

Jane would often pretend to be an explorer, as she had in Ealing, though the grass was much longer here. Once she even found a snake, or rather the snake found her. The bite she received wasn't poisonous, though the resulting screams would have led people to believe she was being murdered – at the very least!

"What's that funny white stuff all over the garden, Mummy?" enquired Jane curiously, a few months later. "Is it snow, like on Christmas cards?"

"Yes, darling," replied her mother, amused at her little daughter's excitement over such a simple thing. "Would you like to play outside in the snow with Mary? You'll have to wrap up warmly and put on your wellington boots."

An early taste of snow for Jane and Mary

What a good idea, thought Jane. Straight after breakfast, therefore, she and Mary found themselves actually playing in real snow for the first time in their lives. Later, their mother even showed them how to build their first snowman and dress him up like an old man with a warm coat, a silly hat, and a carrot for a nose.

23

The next-door neighbours were a lovely elderly couple called the Nevilles. When the children were small, the Nevilles' house was, for them, like a second home. Mrs Neville often minded them when Jane's mother was busy.

The Nevilles had two grown-up sons: Brian, who was training to be a medical specialist, and Jack, who was very good with children and who worked as a painter/decorator. It was Jack who was to become Jane's friend. He would make Airfix models with her and show her his old comics, making up stories about the characters in them. In years to come, Jane was to hear the terribly sad news of Jack's premature death. Apparently he had fallen asleep and drowned in his own bath, exhausted after a hard day's work.

In March of the year she started primary school, 1960, Jane's little brother, John, was christened, in Devon, at St Andrew's Church (built in the thirteenth century) in Buckland Monachorum, close to Yeoland House, where Grampa had been born and brought up. This was a short ferry ride from Saltash in Cornwall. The family rented a house in East Looe, not far from Saltash, close to Auntie Helen and their cousin Mary. The family were very fond of "Auntie" Mary, as the children called her.

The family with Nanny staying in Looe for John's christening

In early September, Jane started school. She wore a very simple uniform, which she and her mother had bought at a local shoe shop while Mrs Neville minded John and Mary.

Jane's mother was waiting outside the reception classroom with her when the woman next to them introduced herself.

"Hello. I'm Doreen Ayling, and this is my daughter, Janet." She pointed to a fair-headed girl who was smiling at Jane. "It looks like our daughters might be friends."

Jane (centre) sitting next to Janet, with other friends and family

While the two women chatted, Jane was making her first close school friend. She didn't know it at the time, but she wouldn't have long to enjoy this new friendship before life at school would be rudely interrupted.

CHAPTER 5

Complications with measles

"Mummy, I can't feel my legs," cried Jane. "I'm trying to, but they just won't do anything."

Pam, although quite alarmed by her daughter's obvious distress, didn't want to make things worse by showing her alarm, so she decided to make light of it by suggesting that Jane might just be overtired after a busy day at school and a long walk home. She carried her up to bed, assuring her that everything would no doubt seem just like a bad dream in the morning. She planned to discuss the situation with Jane's father as soon as he got home from work – if he got home! She knew that doctors worked long hours, but not this long; he was hardly ever at home these days. When she heard his car turn into the driveway, she hurried to get him a stiff drink, as she thought he might need one.

Jane's school days seemed as though they might be over almost as soon as they had begun, although her mother hoped she was wrong, or at least that the complications she feared wouldn't be severe enough to ruin her life.

When Peter came downstairs after changing out of his work clothes, she handed him his drink, told him about Jane, and described her apparent paralysis. "Oh, Peter, what on earth are we going to do if these are complications from measles?" she asked him plaintively. They were planning to have more children soon, but that was the last thing on her mind at that precise moment. All she wanted was for her firstborn child to survive and grow up to be successful and happy.

"Don't worry, darling," said Peter gently, putting his arms around his wife's shoulders. "If Jane can't feel her legs in the morning, I'll get her an emergency appointment with Dr Slot. He is a very respected and experienced paediatrician who works at St Nicholas. Fortunately, he has a clinic there tomorrow morning."

The following morning, Jane could neither feel nor move her legs and was in a state of shock. Her mother wrapped her in a blanket and carried her out to the car. The drive to the hospital flew by in silence. Jane was absolutely speechless with both bewilderment and terror. Pam, too, was lost for words.

Dr Slot's clinic was in the new building at the back of the hospital. Pam parked the car next to the clinic's entrance, carried Jane inside, and placed her on the first empty chair in the clinic's waiting room. Then she went to reception. She was told to take Jane in immediately. Once she did, they were confronted by a short, stout kindly looking elderly man, Dr Slot, who bore an uncanny resemblance to Hercule Poirot.

After examining Jane, Dr Slot made a quick diagnosis and sent her directly to the Brook Hospital, because it had superior facilities for this sort of case. Pam declined his offer of an ambulance, because she thought it would be less traumatic for her daughter if she drove her herself.

"We have to go to another hospital now, Jane. You'll have to stay there until the doctors make you better," said Pam gently to her small daughter.

"Can't you or Daddy make me better?" enquired Jane. Tears began to run down her cheeks.

As soon as they approached the small modern isolation unit (for contagious diseases such as measles) annexed to the Brook Hospital, where Jane was to stay, doctors, nurses, and porters pushing gurneys came rushing out to meet them. Later, as she lay in a bed in the unit,

Jane was to think that she must be very important to have warranted such special treatment. Perhaps she really was a queen or someone just as special, like a fairy princess …

After the doctors had completed all their tests, Jane was admitted to a large pleasant room in the unit, with its own bathroom. However, after such a long, exhausting day, which was already beginning to darken, she fell quickly into a deep, dreamless sleep.

In the morning, Jane began to notice both her surroundings and what was going on around her. She found she was in total isolation in a room where the blinds were drawn at first. Not only could she not leave, but also she was allowed no visitors, which made her feel just like a prisoner trapped in a dungeon. The poor quality of the hospital food confirmed this suspicion. To compensate, Pam would cook Jane delicious home-made treats of chocolate cake and fudge cake bars, and the family would present them to Jane from outside her window. Small wonder that Jane put on weight in hospital!

She made friends with the girl in the isolation room next door. Without words, they were both able to play and "talk" using toy farmyard and jungle animals. Actually, Jane much preferred using jungle animals, as she found them more exotic. She would also share her mother's home-made treats with her friend in isolation, asking one of the nurses to take them next door.

After Jane was transferred to the children's ward, she never saw the other girl again and often wondered if she had died (she would later hear that several children had died as a result of the measles epidemic that year, 1960, including two in south-east London alone). The children's ward was situated in the old hospital building, and it was from there that Jane would begin her long, slow recovery, starting with learning to walk again from scratch.

CHAPTER 6

Recovery

"**D**o you think they'd let me come home for Christmas, Mummy?" enquired Jane. "I don't know if I'll be able to walk by then, though," she added, sounding rather worried.

"I don't think that would be a problem," her mother reassured her. "I thought you might need a wheelchair at first anyway to return to school."

Jane was mortified by this. Imagine her in a wheelchair! She just couldn't bear the idea of being in a wheelchair, like an "invalid" – and she was definitely not an invalid. From that day on she was determined to learn to walk again, quickly. With an iron will she worked with the physiotherapist, Mr Alice, to strengthen her legs. First he just gave her exercises to do, and then he taught her to crawl, which enabled her to reach the exercise bikes in the hospital gym.

"Just as well they can't move," muttered Jane under her breath, as she pulled herself into the seat of one of the bikes. She worked tirelessly for hours, trying and eventually succeeding to pedal the bike in order to build up her muscles. "Walking" on her knees came next, followed by walking between parallel bars and then, finally, walking unaided!

It was never quite the same, though. Jane found she could no longer run – or even walk very far. People would always assume she had flat feet. Still, it was better than nothing, her abiding optimism screamed – and a whole lot better than it had been for those children who had died.

Jane was home in time for Christmas, although she still had to wear those infernal leg splints.

Christmas was as magical as ever, despite the splints. On Christmas Eve night, she lay awake straining her ears for the sound of sleigh bells ringing, only half believing in Father Christmas at the advanced age of 5, but not quite ready to forget him entirely either.

"I don't suppose people like Mummy and Daddy and nurses and teachers could be Father Christmas's helpers, could they?" Jane wondered aloud, as she and her sister tried to go to sleep that night, something which was always almost impossible on Christmas Eve night. Eventually, though, after assuring herself that she had indeed heard sleigh bells, Jane fell into a sleep filled with dreams of Father Christmas coming down the chimney carrying everything she wanted, and then enjoying both the cake and milk which the children had left for him, as always.

When they woke up, the girls found that the stockings they had left at the end of their beds had been filled with lots of small gifts like pencil cases, coloured pencils, bangles, and small oranges. Mary thought this was all from Father Christmas, but Jane had seen one of Father Christmas's helpers sneak into the room when it was dark and he looked suspiciously like her father!

After a special breakfast, the three children were allowed to go into the front room to open their presents under the Christmas tree. Jane found herself feeling rather sad as she remembered that she had been going to ask for a bigger bike for Christmas and now she couldn't use one. It just wasn't fair!

From then on, the day was as warmly family-oriented as ever, with the children playing happily, Pam cooking the enormous turkey and all the trimmings, and Peter, together with "Uncle" Bill (an old friend from his medical school days in New Zealand), busy sampling all the wine. Thereafter, everyone ate far too much and paused only to catch the Queen's speech at 3 p.m. on the BBC.

Uncle Bill with John

After Christmas dinner, the adults relaxed over coffee and liqueurs before Uncle Bill insisted on doing the dishes, only to break the lot when the dryer fell quite spectacularly off the kitchen workbench! Before Jane's illness, the whole family would go for a walk after dinner, but this year Uncle Bill made wonderful buildings with Lego for Jane and helped the children sort out the pieces for their jigsaws. Pam and Peter relaxed for a while before Pam made a light supper. Finally, everyone gathered in the front room to watch television.

"You must know that I'm definitely not going back to school in a wheelchair," stormed Jane furiously. "I couldn't bear people pitying me!"

Pam, even though quite used to her daughter's insistent stubbornness, was close to running out of patience. Because Jane obviously couldn't yet walk well enough to return to school, Pam and Peter had decided, with the doctors and the school, that she would have home tuition, along with more physiotherapy on an outpatient basis, and then return to school properly in September.

Pam explained all this to Jane, whose only response was, "Well, at least I won't be at school in a wheelchair!"

Actually, Jane did return to school a few days before the school broke up for the summer holidays, although it was only to ensure that she was able to manage the school day and the classroom which the second years were going to occupy in September, just under two months away!

Jane found that she was becoming rather bored at home, although she was equally scared of being pitied for her inability to walk very far or run. However, much to her surprise, no one seemed to even notice.

Sadly, Janet would no longer be in the same year as Jane, because she had already turned 5 the previous September. The two girls still remained very friendly, though, and their mothers had become close friends. "Auntie" Doreen was in fact to become part of the family in a way, but the family's forthcoming holiday abroad was strictly for the five of them.

Peter takes John, Mary, and Jane to feed the pigeons at Trafalgar Square

CHAPTER 7

Port de la Selva

"Don't you think we should get going soon?" enquired Jane impatiently, eager to start their much longed-for holiday. "We might miss the ferry."

Pam, though in silent agreement with her daughter, was quick to reassure her. "I'm sure your father won't be much longer. We don't want to have burglars getting into the house while we're away."

The three children had been awakened in the dark in the middle of the night to allow for an early start – not that they had found it easy to sleep given their excitement. Pam had then ensured that they were all dressed comfortably and given their breakfast, while Peter packed the car. Before they left to go anywhere, he would spend ages checking and rechecking that everything was secure – so long, in fact, that everyone would start to make grumbling noises and lose patience with him – until, eventually, the long-awaited holiday could begin.

The three children had a great time on the ferry, gazing out over the ocean. Jane couldn't help thinking about New Zealand. Would she have become so ill there? She would never know, but it would be nice to be able to become anyone she wanted to be, even a famous ballerina like Anna Pavlova, whom Nanny had actually seen in her youth.

Unfortunately, all of this only served to remind Jane of her mother's wonderful pavlova cake, a lovely meringue-based dessert, named after

Anna Pavlova, stuffed with freshly whipped cream, and topped with summer strawberries. Perhaps it was not a very good idea to dwell on this right now, though, given her tendency for seasickness!

Jane was feeling decidedly queasy by this time, so Pam thought she'd be better in the inner seating area with her dad and baby John.

When they arrived in Calais, Peter collected the car and the family began the long journey through France.

Jane spent most of the journey looking out the window at the passing farms, animals in fields, houses, and small villages with growing fascination. It was all so unlike England somehow, as though she were living in a fairy tale or hundreds of years ago. All the houses looked just like those in her Hans Christian Andersen fairy-tale book.

Then she saw a field with several horses in it and she remembered hearing that French people ate horses, something she thought quite disgusting. Horses were lovely! She remembered "Auntie" Mary leading her along on a Dartmoor pony. That had been the best thing she'd ever done. She was going to learn to ride her own pony one day!

Jane and Mary admiring the ponies on Dartmoor

As their journey progressed, the family occasionally played games which involved picking out things beginning with certain letters, such as *s* for "sun" or *t* for "tree". Sometimes one of the children, particularly Mary (with her then lisp), would mistakenly assume that a word such as *river* began with a *w*. There was also the game where you had to be the first to find a certain thing. That was how they came to find places to buy things to make a picnic lunch.

The children were tremendously fussy about what they would eat and drink. Peter would spend ages trying to find orange juice that wasn't fizzy and butter that was salty. They eventually managed to make a picnic of fresh French baguettes which were still warm from having been baked that very morning; fresh French cheese, which mustn't be at all mouldy, because the children wouldn't touch blue cheese (not even the slightest bit blue); ham or a tin of sardines (the latter being Jane's favourite at the time); eggs, which Pam would hard-boil on their small gas camping stove; tomatoes; and lettuce. They finished with peaches, probably grown in the little orchard next to their car. Altogether it was a veritable feast! Jane thought so anyway.

Afterwards, Peter told the children stories while Pam drove the car. He told them stories about his favourite cartoon character, the short-sighted Mr Magoo! He would be on holiday in Spain and would introduce the phrase, "Only mad dogs and Englishmen go out in the midday sun!"

This caused Mary to pipe up anxiously, asking, "Are there lots of mad dogs in Spain?"

It was Jane who decided to answer: "Oh, don't be silly, Mary. There aren't any mad dogs anywhere!"

Pam would have loved to be able to correct her daughter, who was becoming a bully, but she didn't say anything. She had recently seen a film in which someone had described a rabid dog as a "mad dog" and she didn't want to upset the children by explaining this, seeing as rabies was still a major problem on the Continent. She just prayed they wouldn't encounter any rabid animals on holiday.

It was getting dark when the family found somewhere to stay for the night. They had meant to stay overnight earlier in a pretty fishing village, but all the hotels were full up because it was the height of the fishing season.

On enquiring at a roadside restaurant for somewhere to stay overnight, Peter was directed to a holiday home only three doors away belonging to the restaurant owners. The place had a single cold tap for the family to share, a Calor gas stove for Peter to heat up water for his shave in the morning, and a handy outside toilet down the garden path. In the house there were large rooms and enormous double beds with soft feather mattresses to sink into. The children loved jumping up and down on them as if they were trampolines.

In the morning, the proprietors made up a packed lunch for the family and even warmed baby John's milk for Pam and put it in a flask for the journey.

After a late lunch, which was tasty but could not quite match the feast they'd made themselves the day before, they eventually reached the Pyrenees.

"You told us the beach we're staying at is over some mountains. Are we nearly there yet?" enquired Jane excitedly.

"Yes," replied Pam, who was now sitting in the passenger seat holding John.

"Port de la Selva is just over these mountains. They're called the Pyrenees, and they're very steep and difficult to drive over. Please, could you all do your best to stay quiet, to help Dad concentrate on the road?" she added.

The next hour proved to be one of the most exciting and, at the same time, most terrifying of Jane's short life.

As the car swung round the narrow winding mountain roads, it seemed as though Jane's entire family would end up falling straight into the ocean, as there appeared at every turn to be nothing between them and the abyss. After hours – at least that's what it felt like to her – they saw below them a pretty little fishing village with a wide sandy beach around the bay, like a crescent moon.

"Well, here we are at last!" announced Pam to her excited offspring. "This is Port de la Selva!"

As the family approached the village, they found that it wasn't as small as they'd first thought. The apartment that Peter had rented was on the second floor. Jane found the stairs difficult to climb at first. It wasn't in front of the long sandy beach, but a bit further back, overlooking a rustic square with a small tree-lined garden, where an old woman, dressed entirely in black, was often to be seen knitting, seated on a solitary stone bench.

On the quay at Port de la Selva

"Can we go to the beach now?" pleaded Jane. "It's not that late. It won't be dark for ages."

Pam, who was already starting to unpack, replied, somewhat absent-mindedly, "I'm sure your father will take all of you for a walk by the beach while I get your tea."

"Would you like me to stay and help you?" enquired Mary, always more thoughtful than her older sister.

Pam was very touched by her younger daughter's words, but she didn't want her to miss out on any fun. "No, darling," she replied, "go with Daddy and Jane to see everything. And take John in his pushchair."

The views at the front were breathtaking! Jane took everything in: the pretty beach, the towering rocks, the fishing boats, the stray dogs scavenging for anything to eat behind food stores and restaurants, even the old *monasterio* perched high on the mountains above Port de la Selva.

It was to become apparent during this holiday, at least to her, that there was something seriously wrong with Jane. She was becoming increasingly unsteady on her feet and seemed to avoid walking alone, often preferring to hold on to her dad, to prevent falling over. What upset Jane most was when the family decided to climb up the hills to visit the old monasterio and she was unable to go all the way.

Jane was particularly fascinated by the imposing monasterio and enjoyed imagining who had lived there and what their lives had been like. She promised herself that one day, she would visit the old monasterio. Perhaps she would be a famous actress playing the part of someone at the monasterio – a beautiful heroine definitely; she just couldn't work out yet which part she would play. She would think about that later when they had settled in.

The apartment was rented and came with its own maid, Juacina, who did all of the cleaning and washing. Juacina was petite and dark-haired. One day she brought her toddler, Juan, with her. Juacina was mortified (and Jane suitably disgusted) when Juan had the cheek to pee from the family's balcony! Needless to say, Juacina never brought Juan again!

With Juacina, the Spanish maid, at Port de la Selva in summer 1961

The children had most of their meals in the apartment, unless they were having a picnic. They soon discovered that the only types of milk available were "treated" (either homogenised or sterilised) and tasted rather odd, not nearly as good as the pasteurised milk back home.

Early every morning, Pam would go down to the local shops, or occasionally to the local market, and buy fresh bread, salad, cheese, and other such essentials, as well as the children's favourite, Ram chocolate milk – a delicious milkshake.

Most days, the family were perfectly content to settle down on the beach, where the children would play in the sand and paddle in the shallow water.

"Of course, when I learn how to swim, I won't need to wear a rubber ring," Jane assured her younger sister.

"But you were very ill, weren't you? Do you think you'll ever be able to swim like Daddy?"

The two girls had put their rubber rings on, the ones with swans' heads in front, which they had chosen themselves and were very proud of. Peter had taken them out for a swim; or rather it was he who had done the swimming, while the girls had looked on in wonder. Pam had taken John for a paddle at the water's edge at the time.

"One day I'll be able to swim better than Daddy," Jane boasted with a certainty she didn't really feel. "I must get completely well soon, surely?"

While the girls were having fun in the water, John was doing his best to avoid a strange little boy who went around hitting all the other children over the head with his spade. John called him "Bubba Bang-Bang", which Jane considered a very apt description.

One day when the family were looking round the fishing boats in the harbour, the local boatman remarked on how bonny (or *guapo*) the "babies" were!

Admiring the boats at Port de la Selva

Jane wasn't very happy about being referred to as a baby: she was nearly 6 after all! But that comment was soon forgotten when the boatman offered to take the family to a nearby beach which could only be reached by boat. It was meant to be particularly beautiful with lots of sand, shallow water, and rocks to explore. There were also plenty of trees under which you could sit to avoid the midday sun, which reminded both Jane and Mary of mad dogs. Much to Pam's relief, they hadn't encountered any rabid animals so far. Peter decided to take the man up on the offer. The family found that the beach was everything it was said to be – and much more. They were to spend many days enjoying what had become their own private beach!

Pam and Peter went out for dinner at night more often than not, leaving the children with Juacina.

Although Pam always put the children to bed before she and her husband left, she could neither be sure if the girls would stay in their room nor if they would be asleep. Indeed, while John was too tired after a long day on the beach, the girls would often sneak into the living room, from where Juacina would sometimes let them go out on the terrace, allowing them to play and see everything going on around them.

Port de la Selva certainly came alive after dark. Jane supposed that her parents were having dinner in one of the restaurants facing the beach. Oh, how she wished she could have been there! It would be lovely to have something really tasty to eat (it would, of course, have to be something English, like roast beef and Yorkshire pudding, as she much preferred English food to Spanish) right in front of the sea, with the lights of the village dancing on the waves!

When Peter and Pam returned, all the children would be asleep, or pretending to be asleep. Juacina would of course keep quiet about the fact that they hadn't actually remained asleep. There would be no need to mention the little cakes she had made for the children (in case the parents were annoyed), because she didn't want to lose the extra babysitting money, which she needed to care for her own children. Actually, Pam would have been grateful that Juacina was obviously so fond of and capable with the children.

Jane's favourite meal in Spain was when her mum brought home a whole freshly barbecued chicken on a spit from the local restaurant for the family to have as a treat on their last day.

All too soon, the holiday was over. Jane had mixed feelings about leaving Port de la Selva. On the one hand, it was a lovely place, with two lovely sandy beaches and warm water, but she had to admit to being a little homesick as well. The Spanish food just wasn't what she was used to, and she did miss her roast beef and Yorkshire pudding!

Anyway, they would be coming back to Port de la Selva one day. Hadn't she promised herself that she was going to visit the old *monasterio*?

The infamous monasterio

CHAPTER 8

Back to school

*A*fter the family's first holiday abroad, things settled back into their normal routine. Jane returned to school, where she rejoined her class, which sadly no longer contained Janet, as she was a year older, so the girls no longer had the chance to play together – at least not as often. Janet now had her own friends, and Jane had to start again, almost as the new girl. She imagined the other girls wouldn't want to be seen with a girl who found it hard to walk fast or run, or even play the popular games such as hopscotch. Jane was now in a younger class, and she and her classmates were all at an age where things like playing with someone in a younger class mattered more than they should. Jane still met up with Janet sometimes at the weekends, when they would either go shopping or play in the section.

Jane and Mary in their new school uniforms after moving to Bexleyheath

Mary started school the following year. It was soon afterwards that Jane actually broke John's collarbone, not that she had meant to, but she turned out to be heavier than she had thought and so a game of horsey-horsey had gone disastrously wrong. John had to be rushed to casualty.

Jane felt very guilty about this, but she really hadn't meant to hurt her own brother! Why on earth did everyone seem to blame her?

Jane had her first romantic experience when she was only 7. To be precise, it happened just before her eighth birthday. A boy in her class, Richard, who was actually just about to move, which perhaps explains everything, told Jane to stand against the back wall of the playground, purse her lips, and shut her eyes. He then proceeded to give Jane her first real kiss, which felt nothing like any kiss she'd had before! "Oh, this must be love!" Jane mused excitedly, and promptly invited him to her upcoming birthday party.

"What do you think I should wear?" Jane asked Mary, quickly adding, "I don't want to look too babyish. Perhaps I should wear something of Mum's?"

Mary, who was rather puzzled as to why her big sister would want to look older, replied, "Why don't you ask Mum? But don't we always wear our best dresses to a party?"

In the end, Jane did wear her best dress, but Pam lent her one of her own necklaces to go with it, which made Jane feel very grown-up.

Richard gave Jane two presents for her birthday: a small bottle of eau de toilette, and a small golden broach depicting a gondola, which were both absolutely lovely and much appreciated. The rest of the party went smoothly, with Jane actually blowing out all of the candles adorning her sumptuous chocolate birthday cake in one go, with Richard's help. The only thing that spoilt the party was that, at the end of musical chairs, Jane made the mistake of sitting rather heavily on poor Richard's lap. She never saw him again, and vowed either to have nothing more to do with boys and become a nun or to lose weight! Pam agreed to help her, because apart from her obvious love of and overindulgence in good food, there was no denying the fact that since her illness, she was not as active as she used to be. Pam could no longer imagine the little girl who had won a race at nursery school.

The two girls were both sent to Sunday school, which was just round the corner. They had been christened in New Zealand, and had several godparents.

The family didn't go to church regularly, because Pam always maintained that there were more good Christians outside the church than within its walls, but this might have had more to do with the incident with the Salvation Army.

Unfortunately, the dresses the girls wore to church were awfully itchy, or so Jane felt, which rather spoilt the experience. She did love hearing all about Jesus though, who sounded wonderful.

However, when Mary, true to form, threw up her entire Sunday dinner one week on the kindly vicar's shoes, they didn't dare go back!

CHAPTER 9

A new sister!

"Are you really going to have the baby now?" asked Jane, with a mixture of wonder, amazement, and excitement. Only a few days prior, the two girls had been moved out of their own bedroom and into the back bedroom, the one that was small and dark, where Nanny had stayed before she had gone back to New Zealand and died. Jane was afraid that Nanny's ghost was still in the room!

A temporary helper had been taken on to do the housework and to give the children their dinner. Auntie Doreen was also around a lot of the time, to help out, which was very reassuring. She had become almost like a second mother.

One afternoon, the contractions which Pam had been having for a relatively short time had become so severe that she had decided to call the midwife, who was dealing with her home delivery.

"Not immediately, but soon," replied Pam, who seemed to Jane to have taken up residence in the small toilet on the landing.

"Do you think you could take your brother and sister over to Mrs Neville's now, please, Jane? She's expecting you all. I've already called her."

"Can't I stay and help you?" pleaded Jane excitedly, longing to see a real baby being born, and sure her mother would need help.

Pam, although aware that her elder daughter meant to help her, couldn't help guessing, quite correctly, that she was more excited about seeing the baby being born than about helping. Pam had already decided not to have the children around for the actual birth, mainly because things might go wrong, but also because she didn't want them to be frightened by all of the blood and pain.

"I'll be fine, Jane. You go with your brother and sister and wait next door. I'm sure *Dixon of Dock Green* is on the television tonight. I know how much you like that!"

Soon afterwards, Peter came to tell the children that they had a new baby sister. Jane was very happy that the baby was a girl, being convinced that girls were better than boys. But then she remembered that her brother, John, was a boy, so she decided to make at least two exceptions: one for John and one for her father.

The new baby sister was beautiful. Lying in the carrycot which John had used when they'd first arrived in Bexleyheath, she had a little dark hair and was quite large for a newborn.

"She weighs over nine pounds!" announced Pam proudly. "I've just fed her, so she should sleep for a few hours. She has enormous eyes, but other than her eyes, she reminds me of you when you were a baby, Jane."

Although Jane was flattered to be told that she had once looked like this beautiful baby, she felt that her own eyes were small compared to her new sister's. Still, at least the baby wouldn't have to put up with her "piggy eyes"!

Jane and Mary with their little sister Ann

Pam spent only a few days in the girls' bedroom with the new baby, who was to be called Ann with no *e*, with Hunter as a middle name, which had been Nanny's maiden name. There was a statue, or rather a bust, of a famous surgeon, John Hunter, in Leicester Square in London; he had turned out to be a famous ancestor of theirs. So Hunter was a family name.

Maybe John Hunter was really Jack the Ripper, Jane surmised. *John Hunter was a surgeon in London at the time of Jack the Ripper,* she figured, *and besides, he had a funny look in his eye. No, that just couldn't have happened. There is no way I could be related to a mass murderer!* She resolved to find out more about John Hunter later, when everything had returned to normal.

CHAPTER 10

Cindy

To celebrate the new baby's birth (or perhaps that was just a convenient excuse), the family became the proud owners of their first dog, the adorable Cindy (who is still sadly missed to this day, by Jane most of all). The basset hound that had paid the family the most attention when they all went to choose one was an adorable female puppy – Cindy! – who was an obvious choice.

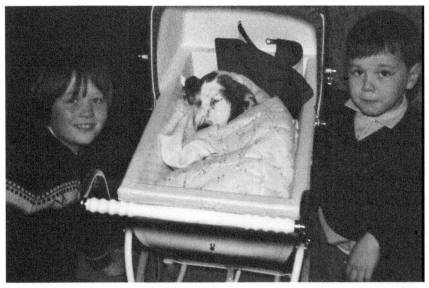

Jane with Cindy (in the pram) and John

Jane had already been dreaming about her ideal dog. It wouldn't matter, Jane figured, if she – because, yes, it had always seemed somehow fitting that the dog should be a female – wasn't very good at chasing after balls or running, because neither was she! Jane just wanted a dog who would play with and protect the whole family, and she would have to look cute, of course!

Jane with Cindy

It was Jane who named the new puppy. She was to be called Cindy. Jane's favourite doll at that time was Sindy, a sort of anglicised version of the American Barbie doll. It may seem slightly ridiculous to name a new pet after a silly plastic doll, but such was the strength of the emotional attachment of an 8-year-old girl to the aforementioned silly plastic doll.

Cindy didn't live very long, but oh, what a marvellous dog she was! She was the only dog Jane was ever able to walk round the local park, and she loved Mary and Jane walking her round the lake in Danson Park, which was just round the corner from South Close in Bexleyheath, where the family lived – although sometimes she would roll in the mud and have to be hosed down! It was around Cindy that Mary and Jane invented "dog language", the girls' private language, which involved slurring regular words in a unique way.

Cindy was very good in the car. Jane often thought of a certain journey back from Cornwall which took thirteen hours. After a short walk before they reached London, where the hold-up was, Cindy slept the rest of the way, curled up on the floor of a heavily overloaded car.

Cindy was also an invaluable companion, both for the children and for Peter when he went out on late-night calls for the out-of-hours doctors' service Southern Relief. Then, she would curl up on the front passenger seat.

"It must be awfully dangerous going to places like Charlton and Woolwich after dark, without at least a gun for protection, rather than just Cindy," mused Jane. Despite having a very deep growl, everyone knew that Cindy wasn't at all fierce. Funnily enough, the only person she had ever used that growl on while protecting the children was Peter himself! That was because she hadn't recognised him thanks to his old raincoat and goggles on a very stormy late winter's afternoon.

One of Jane's favourite anecdotes about her father's being on call involved an old lady who rang him up repeatedly in the middle of the night to tell him that she couldn't get to sleep, to which Peter had in the end muttered tersely, beneath his breath, "Well, thanks to you, neither can I."

A new home

Shortly after Ann was born, the family bought their first home, in South Close, Bexleyheath, having rented until then. Jane found it rather difficult to understand why her parents had wanted to lose the section, the very place where her imagination had been inspired to run free, and to move into somewhere no bigger than the house they already lived in. The thing that won Jane over was that she was offered the downstairs bedroom all to herself. There was to be an extension built onto the house a few years later, for obvious reasons: three growing children couldn't share a bedroom forever, especially when one of them was a boy!

CHAPTER 11

Carry on camping

Baby Ann was to be only 18 months old when the family returned to Port de la Selva. This time, the plan was to spend a few days on a campsite just outside the village. Unfortunately, however, the whole family were to find that they actually hated camping. This adventure was not a success!

All the toilets were dirty. There was no caretaker to help or complain to. The site was overwhelmed and unable to cope. The facilities had not been maintained properly.

Thankfully, late one night the family moved into a house in L'Escala. The house was in the middle of nowhere (which gave it an air of mystery), but it was just a two-mile drive to the nearest beach, which turned out to be ideal.

Peter would drive the family to the beach each day and also into town. The children loved playing on the beach, and Jane enjoyed running up and down the sand dunes.

The house came with a maid, who was very odd-looking, as Jane recalled, with only three visible teeth. She was very helpful and kind, however, and soon took a shine to baby Ann, even though Ann would jump up and down, screaming, whenever she saw the maid.

The family had planned to stay one week at the campsite but decided to stay in L'Escala instead for both weeks. Auntie Mary joined the family on this holiday, as planned. She flew into Gerona. Peter picked her up by car from the airport and brought her to the rented house.

The family with Auntie Mary at L'Escala in summer 1964

There were old Roman ruins on the coast near L'Escala, and the remains of an old ruined city nearby.

Pam and Peter took the children to Spain every year by car for a number of years in the 1960s. They tended to stay in rented accommodation with a maid, as they found this very convenient while the children were small.

The holiday was a huge success, a wonderful break from normal life. On the way home, they took the sleeper train, with the car on it, from Avignon to Paris, for the first time, which the children found very exciting.

CHAPTER 12

Drama queen

*I*n the last three years of primary school, Jane won several medals in speech festivals at school and was even given the job of showing a fellow pupil how to speak clearly. She actually had a very clear voice in those days! The girl in question had an incredibly soft voice with a pronounced lisp. Jane found it very difficult to encourage her to speak clearly.

Acting was something Jane really enjoyed. She wanted to become an actress, though not a glamorous one. Rather, she wished to be a character actress, like Bette Davis, whom she greatly admired for her performances in films such as *Dark Victory* and *Now, Voyager*. Jane Wyman and Ingrid Bergman were also much admired. Yes, Jane would often dream of becoming an actress like these famous stars. Of course, they weren't popular at that time, having had their heyday in the 1940s, but Jane did love to watch old movies on television on Sunday afternoons with a mug of the leftovers of the Sunday roast blended into a wonderful soup. Pam didn't have a blender in those days, so she would use an incredibly old-fashioned Mouli mixer.

It was in her last year at primary school that Jane finally learnt the terrible truth about how babies are made. Janet told her the gory details on the way home from the shops one Saturday. Jane was horrified. She couldn't think of anything more disgusting! She swore that if she ever wanted a baby, she would adopt!

Most Friday mornings, Jane's class went swimming in Crook Log Swimming Baths, which were just round the corner from South Close. She hated the changing room because she had already started to develop physically and was very embarrassed about it – so embarrassed, in fact, that she had started to flatten her chest with bandages for PE.

Jane would claim to have done the crawl and the breaststroke, when she'd actually only managed a kind of doggy-paddle, and even then only one width, with the teacher's son making sure her feet didn't touch the bottom of the pool!

"Oh, that was easy!" exclaimed Jane, sounding somewhat surprised. She had expected the 11+ examination she had just sat to be more difficult, especially because she had recently failed an entrance examination to Blackheath Girls' High School. Mind you, she was convinced that this had more to do with her inability to write as quickly as the other candidates than with anything else. Well, if she passed this 11+, she would be proven right!

The 11+ didn't involve much writing; it was more of an intelligence test, involving a lot of problem solving, the ideal kind of test for Jane.

In case Jane didn't score well enough in the 11+ to go to one of the top grammar schools, she was provisionally enrolled in Farringtons, a private boarding school, as a backup plan. There was no entrance examination to Farringtons. All that seemed to matter was that they liked you at interview and your parents could afford the fees.

"I do like the school and its grounds very much, especially the swimming pool," said Jane enthusiastically, adding vehemently, "but I'm definitely not going to board!"

"You'll probably not be going there," soothed Pam, who was more than a little worried that Jane wouldn't be going to any normal school.

All dressed up – Jane in her new school uniform,
with her brother and sisters

CHAPTER 13

The summer of '67

$\mathcal{J}$ane was nearly 12 and just about to start at her new school, Chislehurst and Sidcup Girls' Grammar,

Jane in her new Chislehurst and Sidcup Girls' Grammar School uniform

when she returned to Port de la Selva. "Auntie" Mary was to join the family in a few days. As far as Jane knew, they – or at least Peter and any child he could drag off the beach! – were to meet her at the airport.

In reality, Auntie Mary was not to join them on holiday this time. She had died a few days prior in mysterious circumstances, back in Cornwall. Pam and Peter had decided not to tell the children what had actually happened until they'd arrived in Spain, thinking this would give them distance and time to absorb the sad news.

Auntie Mary had, it seems, come home early from work one Monday and taken her beloved Yorkshire terrier, Sweetie Pie, for a walk. (Truth be told, Jane had always secretly considered Sweetie Pie to be a terribly yappy, rather diminutive mutt with foul breath!)

Auntie Helen had really started to worry about her daughter when Sweetie Pie came home later alone, without any lead.

Apparently, Auntie Mary's younger brother, Uncle John, had suggested calling the police, because he knew that Sweetie Pie would never have come home alone without her beloved mistress. Uncle John had then joined the police to help them look for his sister, but he had returned with only Sweetie Pie's lead, which Auntie Mary had always removed once they reached the fields.

There had been no sight of Auntie Mary and she was never to be seen again.

The police suspected suicide or foul play. No one knew what to think. Suicide seemed quite out of character. No one knew for certain what had happened.

Jane was terribly upset. She had loved Auntie Mary very much and would really miss her.

The wheelchair

As time passed, Jane's problems with mobility would become more and more pronounced. Eventually, around 1970, a wheelchair was provided for her use at home. Jane was reluctant to use this at first, as her main problem was with balance; she could still stand up and walk, with support or with a walking frame, though unsteadily and with increasing difficulty.

One of the last photos to show Jane standing, at a family
wedding with her mum and dad (July 1970)

To prevent Jane's morale from sinking, never to rebound, Mary and Ann would take their big sister to Danson Park in Bexleyheath, where Jane could often be seen pushing her own wheelchair round the park, with her younger sisters swapping places to hitch a ride. This was wonderfully therapeutic for Jane and helped normalise the chair for her.

It was not until Jane was about to enter sixth form that her mobility had deteriorated to such an extent that, for the first time, she needed to start going to school in the wheelchair. This filled Jane with trepidation. What on earth would her friends think? Would she be accepted? Would she fit in?

CHAPTER 14

Lower sixth, 1972

*J*ane was quite nervous about being seen in a wheelchair at school. She was worried that everyone might see her as a "helpless cripple". Pam tried to reassure her by telling her that she would be able to go out with her friends just like any normal teenager. "In no time you'll be bringing home a boyfriend," she would say.

Of course, Pam was right. As soon as Shael and Beverley saw the wheelchair, they began to plan "Jane's reintroduction to society". Jane had never really been able to go out much, and F had never had anyone to encourage her to. Shael and Beverley had asked the boys they knew if the idea of a girl in a wheelchair still kindled any interest. The answer was a pleasant surprise for Jane! The general opinion seemed to be that simply being disabled and using a wheelchair made no difference.

There wasn't much time to worry. This was probably for the best, as Jane would only have driven everyone mad, worrying about what to wear and how to do her make-up. As it was, Shael and Beverley asked her to go with them to the rugby club near their school, where there was nothing special going on – the best way to get Jane used to going out.

Jane was rather excited about actually meeting boys for the first time. It was one thing to read romantic novels, articles, and poetry, not to mention plays. *Romeo and Juliet* had always been a favourite of hers. And, of course, Jane had had crushes on boys for quite some time. She

62

remembered an electrician who was working in the school and, Jane later discovered with a touch of jealousy, was having an affair with a sixth-former.

The boys who went to the rugby club regularly tended to be given nicknames. There was Tinker, who rather liked Jane, though Jane was less keen on him. There was also Potts, who didn't play rugby, or at least Jane didn't think he did. He was absolutely crazy about Shael, following her around like a faithful dog. Jane was convinced that one day soon they would get married. Then there was British Birds. He was a birdwatcher, who was rather interested in F, who seemed to actually enjoy dancing with him. Unfortunately, like Jeff (whom Jane would meet later), he said he'd see F again but never turned up. There were some girls who were often at the rugby club and had a bad reputation for being "too easy" on the rugby field.

One particularly hot and humid summer's night, Jane, rather foolishly, went out on the rugby field with Tinker. When he asked her if she could get out of her wheelchair, Jane lied and said she couldn't. Jane didn't want to get close to someone like Tinker. She thought he was nice enough, but he never had anything worthwhile to say, at least not to her.

He probably sees me as just a pretty little cripple without a mind of her own, reflected Jane. *Well, if I am ever to become serious with anyone, it will be with someone who treats me like an intelligent human being, someone who I really love.*

Soon Jane met another boyfriend at the rugby club. Because he was rather skinny, he became known as "Tin Ribs". At the time there was a rather stout wheelchair-bound detective named Ironside on TV. Tin Ribs was a sort of watered-down version of him. Jane was 16 (nearly 17), and he was 21. Quite a difference, you might think, but not in the 1970s. They only had one date, and that was to a church hall, where Tin Ribs got banned for being disruptive.

"Will you be seeing Tin Ribs again?" enquired F.

"I don't really know," said Jane. "But he gave me his phone number and told me to ring him on Monday, because he won't be working then.

The only problem is that I hate making any phone calls," she added, with a touch of embarrassment.

"Oh, don't tell me Tin Ribs actually has a job!" marvelled Shael. "What does he do?"

"Something to do with public health, I think he said," replied Jane.

"Probably a dustman, then, or a road sweep," mused F.

Other girls Jane's age would always spend ages and ages chatting on the phone. She supposed her aversion to it had something to do with this Friedreich's ataxia or maybe even her old myeloencephalitis. Her trouble with the phone seemed to go back a very long time, though she distinctly remembered her mother saying she was very good on the phone when she was 3 or 4.

The four girls snuck out of school as soon as the lunch bell sounded. They made their way to the phone booth nearest to the school. Jane was considerably relieved when Tin Ribs himself answered, almost straightaway, and the actual phone call turned out to be thankfully brief. She hadn't really intended to give him her address, but they agreed to meet up at her house that weekend. Jane would have much rather gone out, but she supposed the wheelchair would make that difficult. Oh, that infernal wheelchair!

"See, that wasn't too bad, was it?" said Beverley, after Jane put down the phone.

"It was easy, but I don't know what my family will make of him," replied Jane. "And I don't know what to do with him all evening."

"Oh, Jane, I'm sure you'll think of something!" cried Shael. "It's not that difficult!"

Jane was nearly 17 when Tin Ribs presented her with a St Christopher medal, in real silver, on a silver chain. Of course, Jane was very impressed with her early birthday present, but she had hardly any time to appreciate it, because the very next day, which was her actual birthday, Tin Ribs dumped her, saying she was too young.

"Don't worry," consoled Beverley, "I'll take you out again tomorrow, to forget all about him, and F must come along as well, to keep watch for any teachers, as we're not supposed to leave the school premises at lunchtime."

After being dumped by Tin Ribs, Jane, that very same evening, met a very nice boy called Jeff, who went to a local college. He was the only boy Jane had ever met at the rugby club who talked about books or writing or, in fact, anything worthwhile. Perhaps that is a bit of an overgeneralisation, but nevertheless, it is the way Jane felt after meeting Jeff. She had originally gone off with him to make Tin Ribs jealous or, at least, to make him regret having dumped her. However, she really liked Jeff – and he wasn't bad-looking either!

Jeff told Jane she was something special and that he definitely wanted to see her again. Jane gave him her address, but for some reason, she knew he wouldn't call. Maybe it was the wheelchair, or maybe it was just that Jeff seemed too good to be true.

After that night, the night of her birthday, Jane sank into a very normal state of depression. Everyone assumed it was because of Tin Ribs, but Jane alone knew the real cause. Of course, she could have confided in F, but it seemed to be a bit silly, so instead she would shut herself in her bedroom and play her favourite record over and over again. That record was, most appropriately, "In a Broken Dream" by Python Lee Jackson, sung by Rod Stewart.

Jane continued to go to the rugby club on a fairly regular basis for the next two years, but she didn't find another boyfriend. Jane was worried she would end up a spinster, with no life of her own.

CHAPTER 15

Stirling, 1976

*J*ane had only been at Stirling University for a few days when she first met the boy who was to become so very important to her, so dearly loved, her true soulmate. But that was yet to come. For the moment he was just a boy doing economics, and Jane was just a disabled girl doing psychology.

One Friday afternoon in early March, Jane met the boy doing economics again, and this time he was to change her life forever.

She had gone to visit her friend Pam, who was resting in her room, having been given a week off classes for medical reasons.

On entering Pam's room, Jane found her having coffee with two boys, one being Robin, whom she already knew, as he was doing sociology with her, and the other being the boy doing economics whom she had met right at the beginning. Only now he appeared somehow different, more interesting. His name, which she hadn't caught that first time, was Alan Maxwell.

Alan seemingly found economics, which his dad had persuaded him to study, dead boring. He had even been talked into studying accountancy for one semester, but he had, most conveniently, fallen asleep during the examination. He much preferred English and German, which he had switched to, though his first love was music. Alan had actually been in a band just before coming to university. He and his band had reached the final of a national rock music competition broadcast on the radio. *Wow! Exciting stuff!*

Jane listened, enthralled, to Alan's soft lilting Scottish accent. Together with his enormous dark eyes … well, there was nothing that could have prevented her from falling deeply in love with him!

Alan (Prestwick, 1976)

Pam must have sensed something, because she invited Robin and Alan to go to the pub just off campus the following night, with her and Jane, and another friend, Helen, whose room was down the corridor from theirs. *O bliss! Another chance to see Alan!*

Jane took an incredibly long time to get dressed for her evening at the pub – nearly all day, in fact. She had decided to wear her knee-high boots because they made her look less disabled, supporting her ankles better and stopping them from falling to one side. This was very important to her, because she hated being different. More importantly, would Alan mind her being different?

At the pub Jane had her usual vodka and lime, completely forgetting how expensive it was compared to the lager the others were drinking. The evening was very successful, with lots of lively and amusing conversation and observations, like the fact that Robin's brother looked remarkably like Elvis Presley, something which normally would have made Jane desperate to meet him, but she could only think of Alan!

Finally, having had far too much to drink, Jane fell asleep on Alan's shoulder and awoke later to a delicious feeling of warmth, safety, and – could it be? – love. *No,* she decided, *it's just wistful thinking. I'm not that lucky!*

Jane hadn't told anyone about her feelings for Alan, which was just as well, because the following afternoon, Penny, a girl in the same year, admitted to Pam and Jane that she had fallen for Alan. *Oh no,* thought Jane. *Penny's so quiet and shy. He may not have noticed her yet, but he's sure to prefer her to me, as she's not disabled.*

However, Jane hadn't given up entirely. She remembered all too clearly waking up on Alan's shoulder and the way it had made her feel.

Penny asked Pam if she could help bring her and Alan together. For once, Jane was glad to be disabled, useless. Pam suggested they all go to a local pub on Friday, where she would ensure that Penny sat next to Alan. Jane wasn't looking forward to Friday, watching Penny and Alan getting to know each other.

The following week she saw more of Alan than usual, which was, of course, absolutely wonderful, but when he turned up at the same table in the canteen, Jane was afraid he'd been put off by her messy eating.

Pam knew her friend had fallen for someone. She just wasn't sure who it was, proceeding to go through a list of all the boys they knew, until Jane admitted it was Alan, while adding miserably, "But Penny has probably got a better chance than I have," to which Pam replied, "Don't be so sure …"

On the Friday evening, Alan actually pushed Jane's wheelchair to the pub, much to her delight. She told him all about London and volunteered to show him all around, any holiday he wanted. Once they had settled into their table at the pub, Penny found that she wasn't sitting next to Alan but, as Pam told her later, had been placed directly opposite, which was very nearly as good.

Jane avoided looking at either Alan or Penny all evening, feeling jealous, sure that they were getting to know each other. She was introduced to the delicious, mild, and creamy advocaat and lemonade. She would have become disastrously drunk if she'd drowned her sorrows in her usual vodka and lime, so, as it turned out, it was a good thing her drink was milder and more diluted.

Robin pushed Jane's wheelchair back from the pub. Jane presumed Alan wanted to be alone with Penny. Robin pushed her very fast, which she enjoyed. It helped keep her mind off Alan and Penny.

After a brief visit to Airthrey Castle to collect a pen that Robin had left beside the grand piano he sometimes played there, Robin pushed Jane straight to Pam's room, where everyone else already was. Horror of horrors! Jane had been desperate to go to her own room. However, it soon became obvious that Alan and Penny weren't together. Oh, the relief was enormous! Maybe, just maybe, her disability wasn't going to ruin everything for her. The conversation was lively. Jane told everyone about the sights on her recent visit to the south of Italy, including the stray Pompeian cat that seemed to have been around since the very date of the eruption of Vesuvius.

Robin eventually left to see someone else. Jane seized the opportunity to sit next to Alan, claiming to be uncomfortable in her wheelchair. After Helen went to bed, Alan put his arm round Jane's shoulder, at which point Penny stormed out, followed by Pam, who said she was going to make sure that Penny was all right.

That left Alan and Jane alone at last. Alan put his hand under her chin, and their lips met in the most long-awaited, delicious kiss.

"Wow, where did you learn to kiss like that?" exclaimed Alan a few moments later.

"That's my secret," replied Jane mysteriously, not wanting to spoil everything by admitting that it had probably been at the rugby club near her school.

Afterwards they went to Jane's room, not wanting the night to end, and just cuddled all night long, content to lie in one another's arms until the sun rose.

Then Alan went up to his own room for appearance's sake and a change of clothing, wasting no time, not wanting to stay away any longer than he had to, eager to get back to be with Jane.

Jane found herself going around in a kind of daze. Alan said later that he too had been on cloud nine for quite some time. He had even stopped smoking for over two weeks without trying (though he was to stumble with nicotine and not stop smoking properly for a number of years).

Alan and Jane were rarely apart in the weeks before the Easter break. They went up to Airthrey Castle again to hear Robin play the grand piano, which was lovely. Mind you, the best thing by far was when Alan carried Jane up to his own room to let her hear a recording of the song which he said he'd written for her long before they'd even met. It was called "Haunted". Jane loved its beautiful melody. *Imagine having such a wonderful song written just for me,* she thought. *I must be very special to Alan!*

Alan, playing guitar with his band, Paradox (1976)

Alan brought his tape deck and sound system down from his room so that Jane could listen to music with him. In fact, they spent most of their free time together, listening to music. Not that they had exactly the same taste, Alan preferring progressive rock, in particular, bands like Yes and early Genesis, whereas Jane much preferred Elvis Presley and Diana Ross – although they both loved Neil Young and Elton John. On balance, though, Jane tended to like particular songs most, rather than singers as such. For instance, she liked "The Wonder of You" by Elvis Presley, which she secretly hoped Alan would one day be able to sing to her. (Alan found this amusing, as he had not rated his own singing prowess.) The lyrics sounded like "put your little hands in mine", which always made Jane laugh, because she thought she had big hands!

Then came the Easter break. How would they manage being apart for a whole week?

They decided they weren't going to tell their parents much. It was early days yet, and besides, there was the vexed problem of Jane being in a wheelchair. No parents were going to like the idea of their son being romantically involved with a girl in a wheelchair, Jane thought.

Alan carried Jane on to the London-bound train. "See you soon, pet," he whispered hurriedly, in case the train departed with him still on board.

Jane was going to spend the week in Cornwall with her family, something which she usually enjoyed, but this time, she just missed Alan. The fact that Mary's boyfriend was staying with the family only made matters more difficult for her. Jane would lie in her bed and try to imagine Alan next to her, something which was almost impossible because the real thing was so new.

A few weeks later, Jane bought Alan his first pair of jeans at the Student Union shop on campus. He said he'd always wanted some jeans, so it seemed the ideal birthday present. Alan was just turning 19, which made Jane feel a bit like a cradle-snatcher at the advanced age of 21.

One Saturday afternoon, while Alan was at a meeting about his upcoming work experience in Germany, Jane went with Helen to the local vicarage, for tea with the vicar. Not that Jane went to church then; indeed, she was still inclined to wheel herself around shouting, "I hate vicars!" after having too much to drink. It was simply because the vicar was well-known for his sumptuous afternoon teas. She normally spent Saturday afternoon with Alan, so this would show him!

Alan's 19th birthday party was held in the room usually reserved for billiards at one side of Murray Hall.

"Oh, this is cool!" exclaimed Alan, seeing the invitingly decorated room with a table stacked high with progressive rock LPs; his guitar; and another table overflowing with delicious snacks and a generous supply of lager.

"I'm glad you like it, darling," admitted Jane, with an overwhelming sense of relief. "The girls on my floor have been marvellous. They've even helped me bake you a mouth-watering chocolate cake for later," she added, always being the first to spoil a surprise. "There'll probably be dancing after a while. You must dance with someone. I don't mind, honestly," Jane lied, knowing she would be devastated if Alan danced with someone else. She needn't have worried, because Alan refused to dance with anyone if Jane wasn't involved.

Finally, after dancing by himself a few times, he picked Jane up into his arms, twirling around the dance floor with gusto. Although she found this very romantic, she couldn't resist saying, "Put me down, you idiot! You'll break your back. I've eaten too much of your delicious cake!"

CHAPTER 16

The summer of '77

Since Alan was spending the summer holidays in Germany, Jane thought that, even though it was a working holiday, it would be a good chance for her to see a bit more of the world, something she had always wanted to do.

She decided to contact her old school friend F, the one whose original nickname no longer applied, but the initial held the same uniqueness as its owner. She and F both loved Italy. Even though Jane had been twice before, she really wanted to see Rome this time. Why? She could imagine she was a beautiful Christian being fed to the lions the next day, only she would be saved just in time by a handsome gladiator. Honestly, you'd think she was a child again, but it showed how long it was since she had first wanted to see Rome.

Jane got some travel brochures from the Student Union shop, but this time they weren't good enough. She went to the porter's desk to phone F because it was much easier to wheel into than an ordinary phone booth. F was coming with her boyfriend, Alan. Oh, how Jane wished her own Alan was going too! Jane remembered that Helen had wanted to see Italy. And since they had become such good friends and Jane felt comfortable with her (something very important, considering how much she was going to miss Alan), she decided to ask Helen to join them. Helen was delighted. The two young women agreed to meet up a few days before they flew out so that Helen could meet Jane's family and see a bit of London first.

Jane and Alan made sure that they would remain together in the same hall of residence (each year most of the students either went to other halls or to flats on campus, or found their own lodgings off campus). The ballot was organised by the wardens of Murray Hall, so they must have forgiven Alan his nocturnal visits to the female wing.

Alan was to meet Jane's parents before the end of the spring semester. They all seemed to get on really well, as Jane had known they would. After all, who could fail to like Alan? And besides, her mum had always been so proud of her Scottish ancestry. No doubt they would invite Alan to stay with the family before he went to Germany.

So Jane went home with her parents with a heavy heart, already missing Alan as soon as they left the campus. Luckily, it would not be long until the two of them would see each other again, though the summer that followed would be the longest time they'd ever been apart ...

"You'll take me to Euston to meet Alan, won't you, Dad?" pleaded, or rather, demanded Jane, desperately impatient to see Alan before he went to Germany. *You never know what could happen there,* she mused inwardly, *who he might meet, perhaps a pretty, curvaceous German girl who isn't disabled! It just isn't fair!*

"Hi, sweetheart. Look who I've brought to meet you!" said a familiar Scottish accent, and there was Alan, holding out a rather strange kind of snotty-looking furry dog. This unlikely creature soon became one of Jane's favourite stuffed animals. "He can keep you company while I'm in Germany!"

Alan and Jane with George Edward (summer of 1977)

Jane took the dog with an enthusiasm she didn't really feel. Nobody would compensate for Alan, and certainly not a stuffed animal.

"Oh! Thank you, darling. I think I'll call him George Edward. I think that name suits him somehow."

When they got back to South Close, Alan met the rest of the family.

Pam had put him in Ann's bedroom, maybe to stop any hanky-panky (as she called going into your partner's bedroom at night for a crafty good-night kiss). There was also the squeaky stair to contend with, which would alert Pam of anyone going downstairs, where Jane's bedroom was, though they could always say that they were thirsty and needed a drink. Ann's bed was a small bed, made especially for her small bedroom, so Alan's feet stuck out past the bottom of the bed, which proved to be a recipe for disaster.

Jane's elderly cat, Heloise, who, having become a family cat, was now known by the most inappropriate name of "Titty-wits", disgraced herself by peeing all over Alan's feet the very first night he was in the house.

Jane with Heloise, or "Titty-wits"

It's a wonder Alan wants to stay here anymore, thought Jane, *but I'm sure he understands that poor Elou probably got shut in or mistook him for an intruder.*

The following day was a Saturday. Jane had decided to take Alan to London, where they could see the latest films and have dinner at the top of the Post Office Tower.

Alan was to have the pleasure of meeting Jane's paternal grandmother, Ganygan, at Sunday dinner, a rather grand affair in her home. Ganygan, who was profoundly senile, or so Jane imagined, would probably think that Alan was an Indian servant, just as she had Mary's boyfriend. However, when she was introduced to Alan, she was remarkably civil, which, Jane later realised, only indicated that she must have thought that he was her faithful Scottish servant and friend, John Brown, as she seemed frequently to think that she was Queen Victoria.

All too soon, it was time for Alan to leave for Germany, so it was a very forlorn Jane who accompanied Alan to Victoria Station in her family car. She didn't know whether she would ever see Alan again, though something told her that she and Alan had been made for each other.

The long summer holidays had never seemed so long. The days were endless and intolerably boring. Alan wrote as often as he could – remarkably often, considering how long and hard his work was.

Alan was working as a nursing assistant in a geriatric ward, where he was a great favourite of the old women patients. Jane loved hearing all about their antics. There was one old woman who was convinced that her husband (who had been dead for several years) was at the window, even though she was on the fifth floor. There was also the old lady with continence issues who refused to be taken to the toilet at lunchtime until Alan returned from his break. What a treat! Especially as it was on one famous occasion too late, not that it seemed to bother the old lady, who, on the way to the toilet, was heard to cry out, *"Der Schnellzug kommt!"* (Hurry, the express train's coming!)

Alan didn't meet anyone else in Germany, something Jane had feared, but there was one nurse who said she would write. It was a great relief to Jane when she wrote and obviously already had a boyfriend, though Jane did wonder how long he'd been around.

Just before they flew out to Italy, Helen came down from Shropshire, where she lived, to meet Jane's family and to see a bit of London. Jane made sure that they went to Carnaby Street, one of her favourite places, where she took Helen's picture outside a boutique named, rather appropriately, Lady Jane. Smocks were very fashionable at the time; you could find the best ones there. Jane loved smocks. They covered everything – a multitude of sins!

As they left Rimini Airport a few days later, Helen recognised a familiar face at the opposite counter and gave Jane a nudge.

"Don't you recognise that man?" she asked Jane excitedly, pointing at the familiar figure

"Oh, yes! That's Arthur Negus, isn't it? Why don't you go and get his autograph?"

So, Helen went to get Arthur's autograph for both her and Jane. He was a genial antiques expert who appeared on the panel of the TV series *Going for a Song* in the 1970s.

Helen and Jane were staying in Pesara, a resort next to Rimini, although much smaller. Their hotel was right over the road from the beach, which became very lively at night, with music, singing, and dancing, and of course, eating and drinking.

Jane, Helen, F, and F's Alan spent many nights on the beach, where the local pizza was particularly tasty.

Although Jane was having a good time on her holiday, she still missed her Alan dreadfully. On her new tape recorder, she would listen to all the music she always listened to with Alan. Her favourite cassette was by the 1970s band Bread. She would play their *Best of Bread* album over and over again, probably turning Helen mad in the process. On the day the market was held, Jane bought Alan a blue shirt. She had no idea if it would fit him, but it seemed perfect. After all, she should know better than anyone else, after all their cuddles.

The four of them went to a local nightclub, which wasn't that good because you had to buy your own (highly overpriced) drinks and it mostly involved dancing to very badly played out-of-date music! Fortunately, they all enjoyed their excursion to Florence, their only complaint this time being the heat.

Jane was fascinated by the original of Michelangelo's *David* and by the impressive Florentine frescoes depicting the theme of the Last Supper. Although they could have visited Pisa later that afternoon, they much preferred staying in Florence and looking around. After being shown how to make pizza in the morning and sampling their efforts for lunch, and having had far too many snacks, they couldn't manage a single bite of the delicious-looking meal the hotel provided on their return.

Jane and Helen had just enough money left towards the end of the holiday to go on an excursion to Rome. This was to be the highlight of Jane's holiday! F and her Alan preferred to go to Venice, rather than

Rome, something which Jane could never understand, because someone had told her that Venice was very smelly – but she supposed it was also meant to be a very romantic city. There wasn't much point in her going to Venice, she thought. She just couldn't imagine how she would get into a gondola! She'd far rather be serenaded by Alan, anyway.

"The weather's not going to be very good today," said Helen anxiously, glancing out the small window of the hotel room she was sharing with Jane.

"I think that it might be better that way," replied Jane. "We'll be travelling all day, so we don't need the coach getting hot and stuffy."

"No, that's the last thing we want," admitted Helen. "I suppose we'd better go and meet the coach. It might be early!"

When the coach arrived, it was full of elderly German tourists, which proved to be very interesting. Jane wondered why some of the elderly German men seemed almost embarrassed by her. Then something happened which explained everything perfectly – or was that just her imagination? Everyone was asked to produce their passports (something to do with the Vatican being a separate state), and Jane was sure that several of the men still had photos of themselves in Nazi uniform. Hence their evident embarrassment (or so Jane thought). *Someone like me would have been sent straight to the gas chambers for sure!*

When they arrived in Rome, the coach stopped immediately opposite the Colosseum, an absolutely perfect location.

"I bet nobody else is this lucky!" exclaimed Helen. "Do you think we'll be allowed to visit the Colosseum tomorrow?" she asked hopefully. "Perhaps we'll see where they kept the Christians and the lions that ate them."

"I'm sure you'll get to see everything, but I don't think the inside of the Colosseum will be suitable for wheelchairs," replied Jane, with resigned irritation. "You can rarely go anywhere really interesting in a wheelchair! You can tell me all about it tomorrow night, though, and please don't leave out any of the gory details!"

The following day everyone was taken to all the major sights in Rome, including the Colosseum, which had the remains of an old zoo attached, where, Jane supposed, the lions had been kept. Perhaps the handsome gladiator had saved the beautiful Christian girl by getting her a job at the zoo?

Their last visit was to the Vatican, where, even though the Sistine Chapel was being renovated and the Pope was on holiday, Jane and Helen had a truly wonderful time.

The weather was perfect – not too hot, but pleasantly warm with a light breeze. They met two young men from the north of England, one of whom was obviously very interested in Helen. Helen wasn't even remotely interested in him, though. Nevertheless, they all spent a very pleasant afternoon in the Vatican, where Jane threw a coin in the fountain, hoping in her heart that she would one day return to Rome.

"When I return, it will be with Alan!" she vowed with a sudden certainty.

Soon after the holiday, and once Helen had returned home, Alan finished his work in Germany and returned to be with Jane in London. Something told Jane that she and Alan would never be parted again. She was, nevertheless, very worried about meeting him again. Would he still love her? Had he met someone else? Were his letters designed just to spare her feelings? Jane didn't know how she could doubt Alan of all people, but she had so many questions.

CHAPTER 17

The proposal

*W*hen Jane met Alan at Victoria on that hot, sticky day in August 1977, it soon became apparent, particularly to her, that he had missed her just as badly!

"Please, don't go away for so long ever again. I can't live without you!" pleaded Jane, not caring that she sounded hopelessly corny. Nonetheless, she was sincere.

Alan was to stay with Jane for a week or so before he went home to his family. University was about to resume. It was in the Silver Lounge, over coffee and hot chocolate, that Alan and Jane first talked about marriage. They initially just dreamed of sharing a country cottage with two stick insects. These soon became a dog and a cat, and then a boy and a girl. They used to lie together on Jane's bed (fully clothed) in the evenings and imagine their life together!

Eventually, when Alan was reminded that he hadn't yet proposed in so many words, he promptly got down on one knee one Saturday afternoon in late August 1977, in their then favourite haunt, the Silver Lounge coffee shop in Bexleyheath High Street. Jane was terribly embarrassed, but at the same time, she felt absolutely wonderful!

Alan must really, really love me! she realised. *Who would have thought that I'd be getting married?*

Jane and Alan, Silver Lounge, August 1977

Jane and Alan kept their exciting news secret for the time being. They alone knew of their plans.

Meanwhile, perhaps sensing something serious happening between Alan and Jane, Pam and Peter decided to leave them with Mary (as chaperone) for those precious few days together in South Close before Alan returned home to Scotland. The following week was almost like being married. Jane and Alan didn't see much of Mary, who was out with friends quite a lot.

When they got back to university, Jane found that she was still in the honours program. This meant a great deal to her, as she had worked so hard in her first year.

CHAPTER 18

Meet the family

*I*n November, Alan and Jane had a few days off classes, so they took the opportunity for Jane to meet Alan's parents. Of course, she should have met the family ages ago, long before they'd decided to get engaged, but she was absolutely terrified of their reaction to their son being involved with, not to mention planning to marry, a young woman with such a disability.

Alan agreed to take the engagement rings off at first, at least until his parents had come to know Jane as a person. Alan was sure that they'd love her, but Jane worried that they wouldn't be able to get beyond the wheelchair.

Jane was also concerned that the family were devout Christians. *Imagine me, of all people,* she thought, *who had screamed my head off at God, wanting to join this family!*

Jane had for some time seen herself as an atheist, following several bad experiences in adolescence. First and foremost, there was that diagnosis of Friedreich's ataxia made when she was 13. She just couldn't believe at that time that any loving God would be so mean to her. Also, there were many people worse off. *What about them?* she would argue.

Alan's parents were actually rather nice. Jane immediately found that she enjoyed talking with his dad, Bob, who liked to argue vehemently with her about most things, even religion.

Jane and Bob laughing (Prestwick seafront)

Jane enjoyed this very much, as so many people would back off from confronting her as soon as they saw the wheelchair. Unfortunately, Bob was a great fan of the detestable Thatcher and her grating defence of freedom of choice. "A choice that depends on the amount of money you have is no real choice!" Jane would say.

Alan watched from the sidelines, smiling, listening to the prog band Yes on his headphones, no doubt. He had no interest in politics and preferred music to arguing. In contrast, Jane enjoyed the light relief of a good scrap.

Alan's mum, Mae, looked unwell at the time, as she was recovering from a recent heart attack. In spite of this, she seemed very warm and chatty, Jane thought, and had a young and pretty face.

Alan's sister, Irene, was a trainee nurse who seemed very interested in university life. She made Jane feel very welcome. Irene looked like a female replica of Alan's dad, Jane thought, but with a tiny waist. Her nursing room-mate, Anne, came one evening to have a meal. The two of them sat next to each other, giggling like a couple of naughty schoolgirls. Jane actually felt older than they were, but, to be fair, she soon found herself joining in.

Bob, and Irene (Prestwick, November 1977)

CHAPTER 19

Planning a family?

lan and Jane had been married for about four months,

Wedding Day (Bexleyheath, 1 September 1978)

when Jane was to finally accept the obvious – that she did, in fact, have Friedreich's ataxia, rather than a milder form of ataxia, as she had for some reason convinced herself of late. The penny dropped in an unusual way.

Jane had been reading an article in the magazine *Woman's Own* and recognised her symptoms immediately. She wrote to her then consultant neurologist, Dr Peter Gautier-Smith (National Hospital, Queen Square), at once, asking him to advise her how likely it was that any child of hers and Alan's, if they were to have children, would inherit the Friedreich's ataxia. (As an aside, Dr Gautier-Smith would later go on to publish over thirty detective novels under the pen name Peter Conway.)

Dr Gautier-Smith had put Jane and Alan clearly, if grimly, in the picture with regard to the likely symptoms and prognosis relating to Jane's condition back in December 1977, upon hearing they were to be engaged. Perhaps partly in denial, Jane had never really spoken of Friedreich's ataxia, before or since, or even admitted candidly to herself that this was what she suffered from. The condition was at that time considered to be so cruelly progressive with little hope of respite or cure that she found it hard to discuss in a positive light. Funnily enough, though, it wasn't the cruelty of the symptoms that caught Jane's attention in the magazine article at the time; rather, it was the fact that both parents had to carry the gene to pass on the condition.

The consultant's reply was a pleasant surprise, considering his earlier, utterly devastating opinion, at Christmas 1977, when he had advised Alan, who had come to see him with Jane, that Jane had a maximum of ten years to live, during which time she would gradually lose the ability to sit without support, speak, hear, feed herself, do anything for herself, swallow, hold her head up, and – eventually – breathe.

Jane had asked him specifically in her letter about the genetics of the illness. Dr Gautier-Smith had now consulted a genetics expert and he reported that there was a very small chance that Alan was a carrier, and an even smaller chance that any child of theirs would inherit the condition.

Although Jane was devastated to finally admit to herself that she did indeed have Friedreich's ataxia, a dreadfully progressive condition in which everything got steadily worse, she couldn't help being relieved by the genetics expert's findings.

It looks like Alan and I could still have a baby of our own, Jane thought inwardly. *It's like a dream come true. Yes, that's it! I remember our dream of the country cottage with two stick insects and two children, a boy and a girl. Mind you, that was before I found out that I had FA* [Friedreich's ataxia]. *Well, perhaps some of that dream can still come true!*

Jane then began planning to make the best of the "new" situation. She had thought she had some kind of milder form of ataxia, affecting balance alone, one which was neither hereditary nor progressive. Looking back, though, it was almost impossible to fathom how she could have missed the fact that her condition was progressive. She had just assumed that all disabled people got steadily worse, nothing more serious.

The first thing that she had to do, rather regretfully, was to give up her hard-won honours position and leave university with a three-year general degree. Of course, everyone would think she wasn't very bright and hadn't done very well in her finals. Well, too bad! All that mattered now was that she could have the baby she and Alan both longed for as soon as possible and while she was still well enough. She might die before the baby was grown up, but Jane was sure Alan would be a wonderful parent, even if he were to lose her to the illness.

Jane on Graduation Day (June 1979)

As much as she hated to think of Alan marrying again if something happened to her, she realised that he would be too young not to need someone else to share his life with. And besides, the baby would need a mother.

CHAPTER 20

Tiny feet

*A*lmost three years to the day from the day they had first got together (on April Fool's Day 1977), Alan and Jane welcomed into the world, on 31 March 1980, the most precious person, the most perfect bundle, they could ever have imagined: their very own son, Johnny.

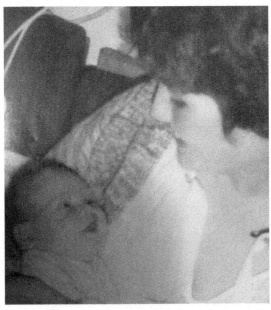

Jane and Johnny, back home, April 1980

Alan would recall fondly, years later, how one of their friends from Stirling, another John, had described Jane's pregnancy at the time as a "nine-month course with a big exam at the end". He would also recall how Jane had passed the test with flying colours and gone on to celebrate with the help of the crate of Ribena that John had kindly given her. Jane always preferred what she called "Skinny Ribena" (or "Skoina Bona", as she and Mary dubbed it in dog language) to anything stronger.

The new baby filled Jane's and Alan's hearts with joy and made their lives complete. His arrival was a dream come true. Many years later, Johnny would grow up to graduate from the same university as his parents, but with a better degree than either of them had managed – first-class honours in English.

Proud mother Jane with Johnny on his graduation
day (Stirling University, June 2005)

He then gained a distinction in his MLitt (master's) degree at Stirling University before qualifying as a schoolteacher at Goldsmiths College, University of London.

Jane and Johnny had an unusually close bond. Johnny grew up alongside his mum and dad, watching as his mum lived through a series of hospitalisations and diagnoses of new conditions, all the time looking on as she grew steadily weaker, though never giving in or giving up. In 2012, knowing communication with his mum by telephone was no longer possible, and so very worried about her deteriorating health following numerous scares involving palliative care and hospitalisation, Johnny returned to his childhood home, as an adult, to be closer to his mum, and to support his dad as the latter cared for Jane. The previously doted-on newcomer with the tiny feet back in student days had become a wonderful support to his parents when they needed help most.

PART II

Jane's Other Writings

Youth passes like the odour
From the white rose's cup
When the hot sun drinks up
The dew that overflowed her.

Christina Georgina Rossetti

INTRODUCTION

*P*art II contains edited excerpts from the written archive of on-screen conversations between Jane and Alan, as well as a selection of Jane's writings and correspondence on other topics that mattered to her. Jane's thoughts and fears, hopes and dreams, and deepest longings are here captured in context, grouped by category. Jane's output during this time period, 2011 to 2016, reveals her perspective on life and events, and gives a unique insight into her spirit, fortitude, wit, and prevailing sense of hope in the face of appalling adversity. Wherever possible, Jane's words have been cited verbatim, the intention being to change as little as possible. Editorial material written by other people, where it occurs, is shown in italics.

Home life

Jane's Christmas newsletter, 2011

*H*i all,

This is actually me. I have not been able to express myself until now. Our annual newsletter will be written by me this year.

First of all, you might like to know how it is I can write this since I can no longer use an electric typewriter and my voice is not clear enough to dictate. I now use a new PC Alan got for me. I use a virtual keyboard on which I am able to "type" with my chin. I select letters by pressing a switch I wear on a chain around my neck. The program was set up for me by Helen, my speech therapist. This takes a lot of patience, which I am just going to have to learn.

Our year got off to a very sad start when our beloved cat Winter, who had been very ill for some time, had to be put down following a fall which shattered many of the bones in her body. Neither Alan nor I ever want another cat, as Winter was so special and had such a lovely nature. I will always remember the way she used to appear on my pillow at night whenever I made the slightest sound, as though she wanted to make sure I was all right.

At the end of May I developed a serious chest infection which was nearly fatal. I'm still recovering from it. Alan has been wonderful to me and does absolutely everything for me. Without him, I wouldn't even be here.

We had to cancel our holiday in Crete, which was a shame, so we decided to get a big TV to go on the bedroom wall. Alan and I sit up in bed every night watching our favourite programmes.

On 26 May 2011, I became a Christian. I once said that I would only believe what I could see with my own eyes. God was gracious with me. On that day, Jesus appeared to me and told me to trust in Him. Although I do trust in Him that everything will be perfect in the end, the waiting is so difficult for someone like me. I will need to ask for His help with that one. I was baptised in the back garden with a watering can! Alan and I now go to our local church, where Alan plays the bass guitar. And to think I used to be known for wheeling myself around when I'd had too much to drink and shouting, "I hate vicars!"

Jane's baptism – with her friends Betty and Dolly (Eltham, October 2011)

We had a very lazy Christmas 2011, which was rather nice, as we're usually rushing around the sales spending money we don't really have! Johnny spent two weeks with us over Christmas. I particularly enjoyed sitting across the table from Johnny and reading my book while he chuckled, talking to his friends on the Internet.

How Jane researched her book

Every week Jane would type out lists of questions for her dad, to probe his memories from her childhood. Then she would ask Alan to write down his responses at Sunday lunch.
Here is a typical example:

12 April 2012

Hi Dad,

I'm working on the beginning of a book based on my life story as I remember it, and I'd be really grateful if you could jog my memory a little, if that's all right with you:
What do you remember about me and the coal shed? (I seem to remember playing there.)
Do you remember me playing with Peter Hillary? I remember it. What did his mother do? And did I meet his father?
Which grandparents was I closest to? What did I call them?
I remember them as Grampa and Ganygan and Grandee and Nanny. Did Grampa have a tickly moustache and a real tiger skin rug?

Typical instructions regarding hair and appearance

Jane had a very close relationship with her carers, who looked after her while Alan was at work. She would maintain her independence by fastidiously typing out to-do lists with her chin. Jane would decide in advance what she wanted to be done and would produce lists or notes on a daily basis to explain everything. She could no longer rely on speech, as it was becoming increasingly difficult for others to understand what she struggled to say.

Here are some examples of Jane's lists and notes to her carer Zoe to illustrate how she maintained her independence, in spite of her progressively worsening disability. These were written in 2012.

Please could you:

- Give me a head massage with all the extras
- Give me a hand massage and a manicure
- Paint my nails using my jade nail varnish with the new top coat and base coat
- Pluck my eyebrows if they need it
- Give me a facial
- Moisturise my feet
- Dye my eyelashes and eyebrows
- My hair badly needs dying. Maybe you could dye it when Alan's at home next week?

Following is a typical list for Jane's carer Zoe, to help prepare for the jade wedding cruise:

October

Hi Zoe,

I'll type lists for Wednesday and Thursday so you can organise your day:

<u>Wednesday</u>

Please mash all the sweet potatoes
Please stew all the cooking apples
Head massage
Hand and leg massage
Facial

<u>Thursday</u>

Cook sea bass in oven with roasted onions, peppers, and mushrooms. Blend all and put in small Tupperware containers.

Manicure

Hi Zoe,

There's lots of cooking and beauty treatments for today, and if you've finished the white skirt, there are a few other pieces of sewing to do before the cruise. There are poppers to do between the buttons on the green and brown skirts, and a cream panel to add to the back of the cream wrap-around skirt – and Angie's still trying to find me elastic for the hat.

<u>Wednesday</u>

Make lots of stewed apples
Make pumpkin lasagne from my new cookbook
Also make me spicy sweet potatoes
Head massage
Facial, and pluck eyebrows
Get my sister Mary a stamped card. She likes dogs.

On another occasion:
Give me another hand massage, paint my nails pink, and put on my splints.
Moisturise my face, neck, and feet.
Change my summer handbag to my winter one, but leave the fan there.
We're going out next Friday, so you can have the day off.

To Alan

Please could you cut my hair tomorrow, but make it a bit longer, jaw-length at the front and shorter at the back?

I'd like the fringe a little shorter, but not any thinner.

There's a strange parting on my right-hand side. I want a full fringe.

Please, could you brush the back of my hair?

Tips for cutting my hair: My hair must be jaw-length at the front, or else I look too fat. Actually, lately I've been wondering if your face gets thinner as you get older. Maybe I would suit it like it was in my 21st-birthday photo? Not sure. My hair needs thinning, especially at the front. The fringe should maybe be a bit wider.

Do you think I would suit blonde hair? I just feel like a change!

I must have my hair cut professionally like in my 21st-birthday photo, but with a fringe.

On Tobii

I really do appreciate the mounted Tobii computer, but when I use it, I absolutely refuse to be treated like a performing animal.

In some ways, it's easier to write now than to read. Reading can be tiring on the eyes.

I don't know what to write, so I'll tell you what's on my mind.

I think I'll write my book today.

Buffy the cat

March 2014

Jane, who loved all animals, all her adult life sent donations regularly in her own name and with her own money to charities for sick animals, to aid the rescue of orphaned baby elephants, seals, polar bears, cats – whatever they happened to be.

It is no surprise, then, that Jane loved all her pets so much. She doted on them all.

A particular favourite pet of Jane's was Buffy, the family's new black kitten, whom her carer Zoe brought to the house back in 2013, to replace dear Winter, also a black cat, who had passed away the year before. Buffy was the sister of Jasper, who was Zoe's own cat.

Here is a flavour of Jane's random musings on Buffy over the years, followed by an amusing little piece Jane wrote during 2014, detailing the occasionally comic friction between Buffy and Jane's ardent district nurses:

When will we be getting our new kitten? I'm desperate to get a cat flap fitted for her as soon as possible!

We've just got a beautiful new black kitten, Buffy. She loves to sit on everyone's shoulder like a parrot! Except mine. She prefers to sit on my head and groom my hair as though **I** were her kitten!

Jane with new kitten Buffy (January 2013)

Have you got Buffy a carrier yet? She'll have to go to the vet soon.

Could you take me to Eltham on Friday? We could go to the pet shop and see about a collar for Buffy so that when John comes to do the trees, she's using the cat flap.

You'd better either book Buffy in with the cattery or leave her with Johnny when we go on our cruise.

Phew, thank goodness for Johnny! Buffy will love him looking after her.

Please, could Buffy go outside to play on Saturday?

If it's too hot, we could stay in the garden with Buffy.

I absolutely love sunbathing in the back garden!

Hah! Buffy was trying to open the window for me today!

Betty was here today and Buffy was licking her nose!

Please, could you put Buffy's cat igloo and her tunnel in the front room for her to play with?

Buffy and Wilfred

When Alan told me that Buffy, my sweet innocent Buffy, actually had a boyfriend, Wilfred, I was somewhat disappointed, until I remembered that she is, in fact, a cat.

Betty met Wilfred (the cat). She was scared of him because he is so big.

What a lovely day. I love Sophie's new teddy. For some strange reason, he reminds me of Wilfred the cat, or at least as I imagine him to be, that is without ears or fur.

JANE How do you know his name is Wilfred?

ALAN As I said, we have no idea what his real name is. Johnny and I just think he looks like a Wilfred. He is a chubby fellow, twice the size of Buffy, with a great big head and odd-looking teeth. In fact, he seems to have two teeth at the front that stick out, and two great big long fangs at the sides that make him look like a vampire! We think he's a bit of a ladies' man. He called again tonight for his biscuits and then went off to play with Buffy. They seem happy. We saw them on top of our shed at one point. Who knows how he gets up there! Must need a ladder!

Then came the curious incident with the intrepid cat and the district nurses, which Jane delighted to recount.

Buffy and the district nurses

On a funny note, a few weeks ago Buffy encountered one of those district nurses who is terribly scared of cats, and the nurse coped very well ... at first!

The district nurse had been trying to check my feet for at least two days, but Buffy had other ideas. This district nurse arrived early to give me my insulin in bed, before Buffy was in position on my knee. So, the nurse shut the door to keep her out, hoping that Buffy wouldn't disturb her. However, she didn't know how clever Buffy is. No closed door is ever much of an obstacle to her!

When Buffy burst in, having pounced with her full weight on the door handle, to give the nurse her due, the nurse kept her cool for a moment or two and got on with her job, even with Buffy in her way on my knee!

When Buffy saw me getting my injection, she extended a paw, as though she wanted to hold my hand and comfort me! The district nurse, thinking Buffy was about to attack, made a hasty retreat.

Buffy was funny again this morning with another district nurse – she always likes to protect me from the ones who are scared of cats. She refused to move an inch when the nurse tried to lift her off my knee. In the end, Buffy gave up gracefully, and decided to take a snooze on the other bed and to let the nurse get on with her job. When the nurse left, Buffy returned, because you can never be so sure what a district nurse might do, and there is always a stream of carers coming in and out to protect me from!

Buffy was very naughty today. She wouldn't get off my knee. Luckily it was a nice district nurse, but even she had a job moving Buffy. In the end, she had to put the duvet cover over Buffy. Later my carers found it virtually impossible to move Buffy.

Lately, though, I think Buffy's becoming a bit too lazy, probably because all the district nurses she's seen for a long time have turned out to really love cats!

To Alan and Johnny

Jane would go out of her way to communicate with Alan and Johnny in her final years, in the only way she could, using her Tobii computer attached to her wheelchair. She always put her family first and made sure they knew they were loved, even when she could no longer speak or hear very well.

I'll start by asking you to sign your Valentine's Day card for me! Tomorrow night can we order a Chinese takeaway? I want mushroom chow mein; tiger prawns in soy sauce; and crispy seaweed.

I didn't think I'd be able to use my Tobii today. I felt so bad earlier. Just shows there's still life in the old dog yet!

How was your day, my boys? Could I have a peach juice and a small amount of porridge for tea?

Let's go to Covent Garden at the weekend. We can have lunch at the vegetarian restaurant in Neal's Yard, and look around.

If the weather forecast is not good, we could go to Bromley, where there's a large pet shop, to get something for Buffy!

Do you think that I'll be well enough to go out tomorrow? I think so, as long as you book a taxi there and back and I wrap up warm. Please, could you write a list tonight?

I'm going to use my Grid 2 to try to communicate. How was your day, my boys? Have you got a music practice at church tonight, Alan?

Which guitar are you playing at church on Sunday?

Next Friday I would like to go with you to London to visit the waxworks. I've forgotten what they're called. I used to love it when I was a child! London Transport would know the best way to get to the waxworks.

Tomorrow, I would like to go to Woolwich! However, I think we should take a picnic. Perhaps you could also take me a warm chai latte?

The way you make my chai latte is much better than the one they sell in M&S, which is too sweet. You should put yours on the market as a slimmer's favourite.

I would like to get some new fabric (not plastic) artificial flowers for the front room in white, blue, and red. OK?

At the big shop behind the arcade, you can get a new kettle for the kitchen and the two picture frames. I want a clear frame for Betty's picture so you can see both sides, and a thin, black-edged frame for the picture of Istanbul, a little larger than the picture, so it can have a white border. Can we go to Savers first for hair dye and then to M&S for houmous?

Do you think you'll have time to water the garden? Thank you! You must be awfully tired after walking home pushing me!

How was your day, darling? Did you go to the pub? I think that yesterday was hotter than today, but I'm not on a train with a lot of other people! That must be awful!

How was your day in London, my Alan? It's not too hot, at last, although Zoe says it will be 30 degrees on Thursday. Sadie's learning to walk by pulling herself along on the furniture. She should be walking after our cruise!

You must be so tired with looking after me on top of everything else. Why don't you take one day off work and spend it in bed?

Your new haircut is very different. It manages to make you look younger without a fringe, something I thought impossible.

You're one of those lucky people who get better-looking as they get older! Johnny as well.

I know I can't be there at the hospital on Monday, when Johnny's having his gallbladder operation, but remember to phone me as soon as he is out of surgery. Just ring two times so I know everything's all right!

Sorry I jumped when you came downstairs, Johnny! I was just so concentrated on my writing. I can't wait to hear all about your new job, your feelings, and your plans for the future. I'm so glad your operation appears to have been a success.

Hi, Johnny, I'm sorry for the length of time it's taken to get this to you. Congratulations on your fantastic new job!

I'd like Johnny to come with us tomorrow, because I'm so proud of him and he looks so good.

Summer 2014

To Alan *on pain, feeling cheated out of a normal life, and the fear of being parted from her family by death:*

I can't speak, so you'll have to wait until I can use my Grid 2. This morning I was sad for two reasons. One, I can't lie in for as long as you because it's difficult for me to sleep with a twisted spine. Usually, I don't mind sleeping longer; in fact, I rather like it. Also, I can't really watch TV anymore, as I can no longer make out anything they say, even with headphones on, and the subtitles are now too small and move too fast.

The main reason I'm sad, however, is because I can't bear the thought either to be parted from you for years (if I were to die soon), or for you to have to continue having to do more and more for me (if I live on)!

It would be so nice to be able to see Johnny happy and settled before I go, and I would love to be able to look after you when you're ill or tired. You may be surprised to learn, though, that deep down I am very happy.

Last night, I thought I was dead. I was crying because I hadn't told you how much I love you.

Yes, I do mean dying. When you're dead, you are no longer with your family. I couldn't bear this, because I feel cheated of a normal, happy life by my FA [Friedreich's ataxia].

I should be looking forward to growing old with my husband after a full, productive life. I know others are cheated, a few even worse than me. It makes it no easier to accept, though I do accept that Jesus loves each of us equally.

To Alan's dad

This email is inexcusably late, I know, but it is very important to me that I thank you properly for giving Alan and me such a relaxing holiday, despite that atrocious weather, not to mention the feast at the Carvery! Please, could you thank Irene and Raymond for all the tasty treats they got me? Irene was particularly successful with communicating with me using my whiteboard.

Aunt Anne and Uncle Bill look nothing like their real age. ... You, yourself, are looking great. No one would think that you've only recently suffered a stroke!

Irene, Raymond, Bob, Alan, and Jane at the Carvery (Prestwick)

Jane and Alan's thirty-sixth wedding anniversary

1 September 2014

What an extra-special day. Thank you! I don't know how you put up with me, and it will only get worse. Next come bedsores or maybe inability to swallow or suck. It might be incontinence, single or double or both.

It's our thirty-sixth wedding anniversary and it only seems like yesterday when I put my head on your shoulder in the pub in Bridge of Allan and felt as though I somehow belonged there.

Christmas joy

Wonderful teenage memories, inspired by Jane's beloved great-niece Sophie's book The Tiger Who Came to Tea, *by Judith Kerr*

December 2014

I enjoyed Christmas shopping today despite the weather. On Sunday I'm wearing my thermal vest. Now I'll finish writing about Sophie's story so we can post this to Lynsey with Sophie's hat and book …

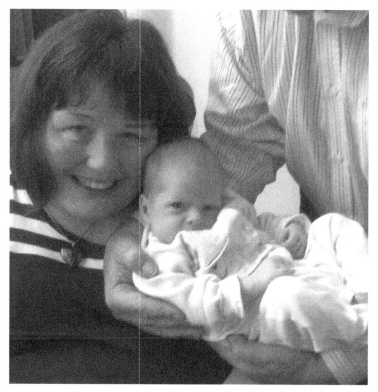

Jane with great-niece Sophie (2014)

First I'll tell you more about the strange coincidence. Before I went to university, I used to work as a volunteer in a local nursery. At the end of each session, I would read the children a story. One of their favourites just happened to be *The Tiger Who Came to Tea*. That was nearly forty years ago, but you chose the same book for baby Sophie today.

I was afraid I might have given some of the children nightmares, as I had made my tiger rather growly.

The children loved the way I told the story.

I really enjoyed working in the nursery. There was a little boy, Andrew, who would only talk to me. Andrew and I would have long, interesting conversations, with the help of the characters from the storybooks I read to him. For example, when one of the characters had ice cream at a birthday party, I might ask Andrew if he liked ice cream, and if he did, where he'd had it and even what flavours he liked.

Ice cream soon became a great favourite with Andrew, who, of course, wanted to know if tigers liked ice cream! I reassured him that tigers probably loved ice cream, not that I really know, but Andrew found all this terribly exciting! He was beginning to talk to other people, to the adults and the other children, especially at story time.

I found working with the children in the nursery very rewarding. I suppose my experiences there helped shape my interest in psychology, which I went on to study at university. I remember now. I dreamed I would be a famous child psychologist, treating children whom everyone else had given up on.

All this I'd completely forgotten. That is, until Lynsey asked me recently what had inspired me to study psychology, which I couldn't really remember, until today when I saw the book you had chosen for Sophie for Christmas, which brought everything back to mind. The book looks almost exactly the same as the one I had read to the children all those years ago!

Great-niece Sophie with another "tiger who came to tea" (2014)

Christmas preparations

I would like you to get some Christmas window stickers.

Please, could you clear the kitchen and keep it clear, as well as your study and the living room, before Wednesday? That's part of my Christmas present!

For Christmas, I would like a red sweatshirt, a red cashmere jumper, a red cover for my feet, some short warm winter nighties, and no chocolate.

My fringe needs trimming. On Christmas Day I'll wear my black wrap-around skirt and the dark pink top with my coral necklace.

We should go to Tiger in Lewisham to have a look round, because we've got to post most of the presents, so they've got to be small and light.

You did well with choosing the presents for everyone ... but you have given everyone too much. They should have only one or two small presents or else all the presents look too cheap.

Check I have everything I need for Christmas. How many cards do I have and how much wrapping paper? And do I have any sticky labels?

Please, could you help me by putting the Christmas presents that Zoe is to wrap in a separate bag with labels attached? She's not to wrap them all, because some are for her.

You will also need to start the Christmas cards. They are in one of the drawers in the chest of drawers in the living room.

Christmas food

Jane kept Alan organised.

How do you feel? Are you OK? This morning you seemed a bit hot.

You've got to do a lot this weekend – the cards, the decorations, and the Christmas food order from M&S. It might be a good idea to do that tonight.

Please, could you get me my splints and put them on? Last night, I suggested Angie could collect the remaining food, including the

Christmas food order. We all eat far too much at Christmas anyway. Well, this year must be different. I'm just so fat; I feel so ugly, I can't bear to look at myself now. You know how depressing being fat is for me. Even if someone gave me six months to live, I don't want to die fat.

Christmas morning

Please, could you give me Tobii tomorrow morning, so I can "talk"? It would certainly be the ideal present for someone like me. You could put Tobii on my wheelchair after breakfast and then put me in the front room.

Do you remember who gave us what?

Thank you for showing me what I got you.

Thank you for all your lovely Christmas presents.

It's a shame you've got to take the decorations down tomorrow. They don't seem to have been up very long!

Faith

Jane's testimony

March 2012

I became a Christian last year (on 26 May 2011) and hope my testimony will be an encouragement to many. So here goes …

In 1969, at the age of 13, I was diagnosed, at Great Ormond Street Children's Hospital, London, with a serious progressive neurological condition, Friedreich's ataxia. I was told that I would never walk again, that I would soon be in a wheelchair, and that I may only have around three years to live.

I did not understand how a God who loved me could allow this to happen. I was devastated. I would lock myself in the bathroom and cry out: "Why me?!"

A few years later, in 1977, soon after Alan and I met at university in Scotland, when we were about to become engaged to be married, we were told by my neurologist that I could expect to live for a maximum of ten years. We set a date for our wedding immediately.

Thirty-four years later, however, I am still alive, which itself is a medical miracle.

Again, last year, in 2011, when I was critically ill with a serious chest infection, I was given only days or weeks to live. I was placed under palliative care and Alan was given the end-of-life talk, told to prepare for the worst, and advised to call close relatives to come home quickly – our son, Johnny, from university in Scotland, and my sister Ann from her home in New Zealand – as otherwise they may never see me alive again.

I was afraid that I was going to die.

But God had other plans ...

Friends and family from all over the world prayed for me to survive and to come to know the love and comfort of the Lord, for me personally. Meanwhile, Alan contacted Cyril and Breda, who present a prayer programme, *Voice in the Wilderness*, on Revelation TV. They prayed, live on air, that I would be healed and would come to know Jesus as Lord. Soon afterwards, on 26 May 2011, the Lord Jesus appeared to me in person, by my bedside, and said, "Trust in Me!" (John 14:1). I placed my trust in Him immediately as my personal Saviour (after a lifetime of embittered atheism!). Soon after, I had a vision of His light dissolving all the black rocks I had seen on a previous occasion, when at death's door, and had understood to represent hell. Alan asked me what this light meant to me, and I told him it meant, "I may have a future!" I now understood that my neurological condition was man-made, and that it was not the Lord who had caused me to become unwell. I prayed in faith to be healed "like Lazarus", and all of our friends prayed with us in agreement.

By God's grace, I survived this illness. Our GP said to me at one point, "I never thought I would see you alive again! Someone up there must really love you!" A few months later, I was well enough to be transferred from my bed to a new, more comfortable, reclining wheelchair.

I continue to find it increasingly difficult to speak, hear, or even move my arms. All of my food has to be blended and my drinks thickened. But Alan and I are very much in love and planning the rest of our lives together, with confidence in the future, knowing that whatever lies ahead, "He which hath begun a good work in me will perform it until the day of Christ Jesus" (Philippians 1:6 KJV).

I now attend church with Alan every week (where Alan plays bass guitar in the worship band). I was baptised in our back garden in October 2011.

I have come to know the comfort of the presence of the Lord in my life.

I have prayed for God to heal all those who suffer with Friedreich's ataxia, not just me. I strongly believe that there will be a medical cure for this condition in my lifetime.

Alan and I praise God for my recovery thus far. We now wait in expectation for full healing, in God's perfect timing, not ours, knowing that it is by the stripes of our Lord Jesus alone that we are healed and set free.

Jane

On church

Getting ready for church tomorrow, I think I should be responsible for my own appearance, so I'll give you a few tips which should help you on our cruise as well!

Tomorrow, if we're well enough to go to church, please may I wear one of my birthday presents?

I went to church this morning to ask for God's help.

Tomorrow morning I'm wearing my new white T-shirt; either my fawn wrap-around skirt or my new green front-fastening skirt, depending on the size of my tummy; and my new cross you gave me last week! I'll need my inhaler the doctor prescribed.

Tell me what happened in church this morning. I couldn't follow anything.

Please, could you write down the lyrics for the songs we'll be singing at church tomorrow, because the words on the screen at church are too small for me to read.

With regard to John's sermon yesterday, what are my responsibilities? I don't think anyone can live without any.

Please, could you use your computer to tell me more about Tim's sermon, and about anything else important at this morning's meeting?

Gloria is the little girl who dances for Jesus and for me every Sunday!

In the Bible Jesus speaks of His church, not churches!

People need to know first of all that God is love and that He loves them and cares for them.

Jane loved telling Alan all about her visits from her friend Betty from church.

Betty wrote everything down, but her voice is very clear here, without any background noise, like in church.

Betty was here for a short time, just to give me a head massage! She's coming back on Thursday.

Betty went to the M&S sale. She said we should have a look. She was amazed at how much I can move my hands.

I must have another bit of Betty's Christmas cake!

I wanted to give Johnny some of Betty's chocolate.

Betty was telling me that Chris will be coming to see me on Tuesday!

Betty told me that she took Rachel some of the snowdrops growing in her garden.

Betty especially liked the way I called you and Johnny "my boys". Do you want go into Eltham on Friday?

Betty is getting me a long scarf for my birthday, and bringing round Esme and, hopefully, Chris. I would like to go to Bluewater by taxi!

Betty thinks you'd get too fat if she made you a pie every week!

To Betty

Hi Betty,

Thank you so much for getting such wonderful Christmas presents for me to give to my boys. Our little secret!

I'm afraid I often lose patience with Alan, in particular when he doesn't understand me.

I enclose some money for the presents (I hope this is the right amount). I am so grateful to you for doing this for me.

Lots of love, and thanks again,

Jane

Conversations on suffering

September–December 2013

To Alan *on patience, the will of God, and the agony of having to communicate at zero miles per hour for years on end while sitting side by side:*

I'll take this opportunity to let you know how much I love you before anything else, but sometimes I do ask God why He made me just to suffer like this!

What I was trying to say this morning was that it has taken me a virtual lifetime to accept that God is not responsible for my Friedreich's ataxia. Now, as a Christian, I still find it all so hard to fathom! Why did He allow my illness to continue progressing as it has, with such dreadfully debilitating symptoms, for over forty years?

I know it's a shame that I have to communicate this way, but it may well be an example of what John [our pastor] was saying in church this morning – God is answering my prayers in *His* own way – either by teaching me patience or by saying that my writing will be very important.

On Jane's relationship with Jesus and her sense of purpose

Jane describing the day she met Jesus:
While I was awake, Jesus put His hand on my head and said, "Trust in Me." I saw this as meaning that things might get worse all around

me but I would always have Him with me. If I am to be healed, He Himself will tell me.

There is always an incredibly bright light whenever Jesus talks to me – most appropriate for the Light of the World.

I was so afraid that my symptoms would keep reminding me that I'm dying. I know that I will, but I don't think that Jesus would have kept me in this world for so long, against all the odds, if He didn't have some special reason!

This morning, I sensed Jesus's presence looking after me, long before we got to church! Otherwise, I wouldn't have had the strength to go.

On Saturday, please could you look up that Bible verse from Hebrews your dad gave me and find the "Message from Jesus" Irene sent me on my birthday. The most important thing is the "Message from Jesus".

Remarkably, I feel better, so much better now that it's difficult to remember what was wrong. I think it was only that I didn't feel as though there was anything to look forward to!

My faith in Jesus sustains me most of all, as I know He has a plan for my future, even though I may not be able to see this or understand it right now.

Ataxia and other medical conditions

Letter to her local neurologist

11 January 2012

*D*ear Doctor,

This is just a brief note to give you some idea of how things are going and to ask any questions. I do seem to be getting worse faster than before I was ill. My speech, hearing, sight, and movement are all worse. Although I can still hear volume, I can only make out the odd word. My sight is more blurry and kind of "shimmery". My voice is very difficult to understand, and it is increasingly hard to get the words out, especially when I am tired. My hand movement is particularly bad, although I do notice that just recently I seem to have regained some voluntary movement in my arms and legs.

I was unwell over Christmas, and the Grab-a-Doc doctor put me on antibiotics for a week, just after New Year, because he thought I had a chest infection, or an infection of some kind. I don't feel like I need a PEG [percutaneous endoscopic gastronomy] feeding tube yet, so long as I eat pureed food and have my drinks thickened, which we are doing.

I hope this helps.

Many thanks,

Jane Maxwell (Mrs)

Diary entry

Jane wrote the following diary entry reflecting how she felt about her relatively sudden loss of speech:

25 February 2012

My inability to talk is extremely frustrating and upsetting. I know it is very difficult for Alan to understand me now, and quite naturally he finds it tremendously frustrating, too, spending all day trying to decipher what I say, when until quite recently, this was relatively easy for him to do.

To her friends

March 2012

I'm at last able to express myself again! I thought I'd take the opportunity to tell everyone exactly how I feel. I feel absolutely useless. I can hardly hear, see properly, move easily, or even speak, and I think that is probably the worst thing that could happen to anyone, to slowly lose the ability to communicate. For example, last night, my arm got stuck under me, and this made it sore, but there was no way I could explain this. Alan couldn't understand me, as my voice was not strong or clear enough.

My eyesight is both blurred and shaky. I don't know if glasses would help, because both my parents wore them: Dad from the age of 2 or 3, and Mum in later life. Even if I did need glasses, I don't think they'd stay on my nose, as it's so small, so I wonder whether I could get laser surgery on the NHS. Nothing helps with hearing. I can always hear volume; I just can't make out the words. I really do understand that Friedreich's ataxia is my cross to bear, and although I am strong mentally, I really don't think I am strong enough.

Although my voice, my eyesight, and my hearing are the worst things, last night my movement showed itself to be very bad too. I was trying to move one of my arms, but the other one moved instead. Often, when Alan tells me that I wouldn't answer when he asked me what was wrong, the fact is that while I wanted to speak, the words would not come out.

My Friedreich's ataxia is progressing very fast at the moment. I used to notice that sometimes my vision was steady, or my voice would improve, or something would improve, but lately there has been no remission, only deterioration. My dribbling really concerns me at the moment. It is so embarrassing!

Letter to her local neurologist

15 August 2012

My hearing and my voice seem to be deteriorating progressively – quicker than anything else at the moment. On the positive side, our son, Johnny, is now back home with us, much to our delight and relief, and I'm now able to communicate with him again. I must add that he is one of a very few people apart from Alan with whom I can communicate.

Alan and I are looking forward to our cruise of the Eastern Mediterranean, just before Christmas.

I don't think that there's anything else that can be done about my hearing. My hearing aids just don't work, even on the setting to cut out background noise. Volume is only affected very slightly; it's mainly voices that I find impossible to discern.

My loss of speech is probably the most distressing thing at the moment.

On the positive side, I am really enjoying the freedom to read and write again using my computer with the chin switch. In fact, I am now well into the first rough draft of my (autobiographical) novel, *Forever Yours*!

Best wishes,

Jane

Letter to her neurologists at the National Hospital

28 August 2012

Dear Doctors,

I hope you had relaxing holidays. Alan and I are going on a cruise of the Eastern Mediterranean in November. Do you think it would be a good idea if I took some antibiotics with me? And do we need any inoculations?

I will try to give you a brief description of how I'm doing. The three main aspects of my condition which are really bothering me at the moment are speech, hearing, and dribbling.

My speech is non-existent. My local neurologist, at Queen Elizabeth Hospital in Woolwich, told me that this is caused by muscle weakness and deteriorating coordination in the mouth area. There's nothing that can be done about this, but my speech therapist is working on the best ways for me to use my wheelchair-mounted computer to communicate with others when I can't speak.

As for my hearing, it's now so difficult to make out people's voices that I can only hear people if they speak very clearly very close to me. Volume's only very slightly affected; it's mainly an inability to distinguish voices, or more precisely, words. My hearing aids don't work, even on the setting to cut out background noise.

Movement is more difficult. I can still move my legs, but not very well, and it's almost impossible to move my arms. However, I can still feel everything, even in my toes!

Swallowing is not a problem at the moment, and I've all my drinks thickened and my meals pureed to be safe. I don't want a feeding tube, as I have explained many times.

There's nothing else to report, apart from (1) I have a frequent detached feeling of not really being here and (2) my mouth area feels worryingly numb all of the time now.

Finally, on a more positive note, I enjoy reading and writing on my computer, which I operate with my chin. I'm in the middle of writing a novelised version of my life story (which Alan has already emailed to his Kindle!). I guess that makes me a published author!

Best wishes,
Jane

On the sudden onset of type 1 diabetes

In September 2012, Jane became very seriously ill indeed with the sudden onset of type 1 diabetes, which she was to learn later is a common symptom of late-stage Friedreich's ataxia. The following words serve as a unique record of the fevered writings produced by Jane in the days leading up to urgent hospitalisation.

In the days immediately before her admission to hospital, Jane, in retrospect, had exhibited unusually high levels of thirst, as can be seen from these remarks to Alan shortly before she fell into diabetic ketoacidosis (DKA). It is remarkable to note how, even as she became so unwell, Jane's concern was primarily for the welfare of her family and those she loved.

4–5 September 2012

Before you do anything, please, could you get me a drink? I'm so thirsty. I thought I'd take the opportunity to ask you a few questions about everything that's been going on. I understand that Johnny got on very well yesterday at his job interview. Tell me more about this. Is your father arriving in the afternoon of Thursday or the evening? Could you please clear the workbench tonight, as you've got band practice tomorrow?

Before you do anything, please, could you get me a drink? I'm so thirsty. Could I have cold juice with Berocca, a soup in the fridge, and a yoghurt. I don't feel well today. It's that detached feeling. Angie noticed it immediately. I feel incredibly hot as well. It's very important to phone Gramps tonight and find out how he got on Monday.

Home from hospital

A few weeks later, Jane was home and able to speak again (using her Grid 2 software). She took the opportunity to explain precisely how she felt, and what had been going on in her mind (with a particular focus on the horror of the cruelly obsessive recurring nightmares that had beset her as she was treated in hospital):

27 September 2012

I feel incredibly lucky to be alive and well and writing this (that is, if you can ever call someone with advanced Friedreich's ataxia "well"). I've simply got to record my most recent experiences in a nearby hospital upon diagnosis with type 1 diabetes (following admission with acute dehydration and hyperglycaemia).

The Agency

For quite a while, I have been having terrifying nightmares about a care agency that does not exist. The nightmares had started the night before I was diagnosed with a chest infection a few weeks earlier. At the time, I honestly believed that my husband's work colleagues had persuaded him to hire a new and better care agency (the Agency), which came with additional benefits for him. I must add, before we go any further, that my husband and I are very much in love, and the only reason for my nightmares must have been a growing fear of being inadequate. Hardly surprising, considering my growing disability, which in my mind must have made me awfully unattractive. My husband disagreed with all this, but I was so unwell at the time that, even though I had never had cause to doubt him before, I had become convinced he was just being nice to me, to cover his tracks, so to speak. Anyway, the additional benefits I spoke of included the services of a nurse doubling as a high-class call girl. In my nightmare I could see and hear clearly, so I can tell you that she was tall and slim with long strawberry-blonde hair. (I was to learn later that the face I saw in my nightmares belonged in the real world to one of the young doctors in the friendly team looking after me. In my mind I had been kidnapped and she was up to no good. In reality, I was in hospital and the medics were making me well again, for which I will be forever thankful.)

I must not dwell on these nightmares any longer, because they only upset me.

I've never had nightmares quite so vividly before, and it is as though the Devil himself was controlling my subconscious mind. It seems to me he definitely did not want me to recover. But why? Could it be that he is somehow afraid of me? This does not seem possible with all the able preachers in the world.

Does the love of God shine through my smile, as my husband assures me? I feel incredibly blessed by this. I spoke to Jesus in the hospital. There is always an incredibly bright light whenever Jesus talks to me – most appropriate for the Light of the World.

The nightmares were still raging; I thought they would always be there.

I prayed very hard for Jesus to take me to be with Him. I received the very strong impression that I still had work to do, although I found it hard to see what I could do for Him!

It was just before I came home. The nurses were taking the blood pressures. The nurse who was taking mine suddenly seemed to be a bit worried. She started looking through some kind of collection of charts.

My heart had started racing again. I imagined that I would not be allowed home from hospital and they would put me on Warfarin again to reduce the risk of blood clots. It was all too much to bear!

I prayed constantly to Jesus that He would keep me in one piece, at least until after Christmas. He must have answered me, because I was discharged from hospital soon afterwards and was well enough to be taken on another cruise a matter of weeks later.

Letter to her local neurologist

In the spring of 2013, Jane decided to write to her local neurologist, as she was worried about getting worse, so that the doctor could read her remarks on the day of the visit. Jane was in the habit of writing to doctors in this way, while she still could, now that she had the Tobii to write with, as ordinary speaking was no longer an option, and she could no longer follow the conversation of others, even with hearing aids in situ.

21 March 2013

Dear Doctor,

I'll just give you a brief description of how I've been since we last met.

Things started to go wrong at the end of August 2012, with symptoms beginning to appear that were soon to be confirmed on 7 September 2012 as type 1 diabetes. In late August I was becoming very confused and had for some time been having strange thoughts about things that weren't real. This continued during the three weeks that I was in hospital, but no one could understand what I said, and I couldn't hear them at all. I actually thought I had been kidnapped and someone had stolen or moved my wardrobe, replaced my regular carers, and gone off with my husband!

Thankfully, I was soon discharged. I am now stable on insulin twice a day.

Alan and I went on a lovely cruise just before Christmas of the Eastern Mediterranean.

My care arrangements are as before and are working well. Alan works four days a week, part-time, two of them from home, and we invariably go out on a Friday.

I have had a couple of minor chest infections since we last met, both of which were treated successfully with antibiotics.

My GP referred me to the ENT hospital in Gray's Inn Road for assessment of my hearing and for possible hearing devices. I am to go back to see the doctor at that hospital in April 2013. They seem to think the problem lies in the signal between the ears and the brain becoming scrambled (possibly auditory neuropathy).

I have stopped watching TV, as I can't follow what anyone is saying (they all sound like Pinky and Perky) and the subtitles are too small and move too fast. Alan is looking into what can be done with speech-to-text conversion – to help me to "hear" words by reading them – as I am no longer able to discern words spoken at normal speed, particularly when two or more people are speaking.

Meanwhile, my voice has weakened considerably. Now not even Alan can understand anything I try to say the vast majority of the time. Most of our time together is spent struggling to communicate.

While in hospital I was put on Bisoprolol (1.25 mg daily) as a precaution (as I had atrial fibrillation on admission, while suffering with DKA and extreme dehydration).

I went to the heart hospital in January 2013 and they said my heart is normal. They were very pleased with me.

I hope this helps.

Many thanks,
Jane Maxwell (Mrs)

To her carers

Around the same time, Jane wrote the following note to explain to her carers why her speech was now so hard to understand:

Here is a description of my speech-related medical condition, dysarthria (which my neurologists refer to often). It explains the reasons behind my problems with speech:

> Dysarthria: The person's ability to speak clearly is affected due to weakness of the muscles in the mouth and throat that produce voice and speech. The person may find it difficult to control the volume of their speech. It may also sound flat in quality. The speech sounds may be slurred or mumbled, making them difficult to understand.

It's such a relief that at last my (former) "shouting" is explained, as is my problem with "tone". Alan says he wishes I still had the strength to shout!

December 2013

I will try to explain my atrocious behaviour! I know there's no excuse, but I feel that only Jesus Himself could put up with my life as it is now. It's even difficult to remember better times, as they can make the present seem even worse by comparison!

To Alan

This morning, I definitely don't feel as though I'm "all there". It's very strange and rather difficult to explain. It's like I'm living on borrowed time. There must be a very special reason why I'm here! I have absolutely no idea what that is, but whatever it is, now I understand why I'm here. Things will improve.

I don't feel well. What happened this morning? I thought you thought I'd died, because you kept calling Johnny, who had probably just left for work, and then you heard me and everything was all right.

I have absolutely no voice today, so if we do a list, you'll only accuse me of shouting or screaming at you, when all I'm doing is trying to make my words understandable.

I've just got to do what Angie suggested and get my feelings down on paper. Otherwise I really will go mad. I wasn't crying because you fell asleep but because you seemed reluctant to turn the TV off when I'd something really important to say. This morning I'm sure I actually passed out in church. One minute you began playing, then I had to drop my head, and the next minute it was all over, and I felt very odd, not really there. It was quite frightening, especially since the night before I couldn't hear my own voice or feel where my own hands and feet were.

To Alan *on living with pain and discomfort:*

I think I get bruises every night I sleep on my back in the hospital bed. Every morning I wake very early in absolute agony with a twisted back. Tonight I'd better ask you to turn me towards the door.

The cushion I'm sitting on is not as comfortable as it used to be, and my slings for my hoist are very uncomfortable. Why don't they make wheelchairs softer like my old Vessa electric wheelchair? The metal bits are awful on wheelchairs and hurt my feet.

To Alan and others *on healthcare (2013–2014):*

I'm not feeling very well today, I don't know what's wrong.

I'm beginning to feel better now. I guess I just had a terrible night's sleep, so hot and uncomfortable!

I'm terribly worried about your knees, do you think you'd better ask the GP to refer you to that surgeon as soon as possible, so you'll be better for the cruise.

Dear Doctors, Alan and I are going on a cruise of the Eastern Mediterranean in November. Do you think it would be a good idea if I took some antibiotics with me? And do we need any inoculations?

What did the doctors say about everything I asked?

Things are very hazy. I can hardly see.

I'll try to explain what I was saying. I think I've got a normal cold, but I'd better be careful that my chest doesn't get infected.

The district nurse could listen to my chest. However, I wonder whether I should see a doctor anyway as I don't feel well.

You must get me some antibiotics.

I'm very tired this morning. I had trouble breathing last night. However, the antibiotics seem to be working now, or so I thought. They might start working later.

I feel very tired this morning, probably because I went to bed late or later than usual.

I'm not feeling very well. Everything's blurred and I've still got a cough, although it's not as bad as it was. There's no way that I'm not going on this cruise. I might need more antibiotics though. I'm very tired this morning, probably because I was awake early, all congested. Just now I was not able to get my breath to answer Johnny's greeting. I just can't wait to get my new medicine.

The cough is back. It's as though the antibiotic was winning yesterday but the chest infection is so strong that it's still got work to do. I'm a bit concerned that the antibiotic is going into my lungs. It should maybe be thickened.

I'm feeling much better today. I've still got a cough but I think it's better. Not as frequent, anyway.

I had a bit of eczema over the weekend. Do you think I should have a facial or just lots of the cream on the table?

On Friday, please could we get some expensive tooth gel from Boots. I hate that cheap stuff you get in the 99p shop.

I don't need a "babysitter" when you're out, and I thought I'd watch *The X Factor* in bed, as well as use Tobii to write! You know I don't like anyone watching me!

I'm so sorry I made all that fuss about my roll. Although I've had a lovely day, I've felt very strongly as though I'm not really there, it's like people could walk straight through me! It's terribly frightening!

Letters to her neurologist at the National Hospital:

(2013 – 2014)

Dear doctor,

I thought I'd better give you some idea of how I've been since we last met.

The worst thing is still my hearing and my lack of speech, which I think are connected. They are both getting worse nearly weekly. This is very distressing and isolating, not easy to live with.

Movement is a little more difficult and I'd like to know how someone like me can lose weight and keep it off, and most importantly of all lose the enormous tummy I've just gained.

Dear Doctor,

First of all, let me give you a brief idea of how I am at the moment. This is to show you that I am still worth treating!

I've recently become a kind of celebrity and my local hospital trust published an article on how I communicate using assistive technology with a head switch.

I can still move my arms and legs a little, just enough to help avoid bed sores.

My hearing is an absolute nightmare. There's always lots of noise in my head, but most of it has little to do with what's happening at the time. Most of it seems to be things I've tried to say, which are rarely understood. They are repeated over and over again very clearly by everyone, even the television! The rest of what I hear repeated is mainly things I've recently heard or think I've heard. Again, repeated over and over very clearly!

My speech started to disappear when my hearing got really bad.

They seem to be connected, so I'm hoping that if you can help my hearing, then my speech will come back.

I hope this gives a brief idea of my situation.

Many thanks,
Jane Maxwell (Mrs)

Letter to her GP:

Dear doctor,

My hearing really got worse, very much worse, towards the end of last year. My speech began to slowly disappear as well, which is very distressing and isolating.

There's always lots of noise in my head but most of it has nothing to do with anything that's actually happening at the time. Rather, the noise usually comprises a mixture of things I've tried to say, repeated over and over, very clearly, by everyone else, and things I've heard others say but couldn't make out.

I hope this helps explain how my symptoms are not "normal" deafness.

Many thanks,
Jane

To her Audiologists:

My hearing aids don't work, at least, not properly. The sound is amplified, but the words are still impossible to discern.

To Alan:

Just a quick note to let you know how I'm doing. Please could you phone the surgery and make sure I've been referred to Guy's. I've got to have an FM transmitter. It's fast becoming my last hope for any kind of worthwhile life. The most amazing thing about it is the fact that it actually works. I was able to hear perfectly, although the doctor's strong accent rather confused things.

My FA seems to be progressing quickly at the moment. My hearing and my voice are worse. I can only hear people with voices like teachers and only when they are very near and there is no one else speaking. My own voice is virtually impossible to hear.

Never ask me a question when I'm lying down either in bed or in the wheelchair, because I can't answer! Wait for when I'm sitting up.

I really feel only half alive sometimes. Everything goes on around me, but I'm not part of anything! Everyone tries to include me, but that's virtually impossible for someone who can hardly speak or hear!

I can't hear much now. To help me, always sit very close to me, at my level, and speak loudly and clearly.

Please could you talk to me using your computer and tell me what's happening as well as more about the wedding we're going to?

How was your day? I said to you just before you left, "You'll be fine," but you probably didn't hear me! Tonight, please could you "talk" to me, using your computer, and tell me what's happening, especially with you and Johnny. Could you also tell me the dates of my next hospital appointments?

Johnny seems pleased with his exams. He told me more, but I didn't want to spoil everything by admitting that I couldn't hear.

How was your day? As usual, mine was dreadful! The new carer from the agency seems nice, she introduced herself, but, of course, I didn't hear! She came instead of Emma and Theresa. Maybe they're on holiday or Christmas shopping!

Letter to her Speech Therapist:

Hi Helen,

Just a few lines to thank you for all your help with my communication needs over the past two years, during the period when my voice and hearing have deteriorated to the point where I am now effectively "locked in". I wanted to let you know what an incredible difference Tobii and the Grid 2 software have made to my life!

It's just a terrible shame that the equipment took so long to arrive, as it can be so very isolating not to be able to communicate with people, especially those you care for!

Now, with Tobii, I have a voice again and I can also write down my thoughts and feelings, as well as send emails to friends and family, to keep in contact, and write newsletters about the places we visit on our holidays, and even my own autobiography, which I hope to have published one day.

I am able to take the Tobii with me wherever I go. I even took it on our recent Baltic Cruise and was able to express myself, and to be involved in everything, in a way that would not previously have been possible.

In short, the assistive technology equipment I now use really has had a life-changing impact on my life and it would be no exaggeration to say that this equipment has helped make my life worth living.

Jane with her speech therapist, Helen Day, who arranged the
assistive technology to allow Jane to speak and write again
for the first time in many years (Buffy listening in)

To her friends:

I was also trying to say that it might help if you could switch on
my Grid 2 on my PC so I could type out what I want to say. If there
is anything else you want to know, either email me or text Alan and I
will reply.

Summer of 2014:

My speech and my hearing seem to be badly affected. I'm not afraid
of dying, but I'm afraid of getting worse. My condition is very cruel.

Your mind is unaffected, so you remain aware of how bad you're getting. Eventually I'll be unable to hold my head up. I may be doubly incontinent.

I've been getting so much worse so quickly recently that my only hope is for a cure for Friedreich's ataxia, to stop my condition from progressing. My ataxia seems to be progressing faster since the start of the year after a very cold spell. My hearing's much worse, although they do think they'll be able to help at the ENT hospital. My voice is virtually impossible for others to hear or for me to find.

I was really relying on the hospital we were attending to improve my hearing and speech – some hope, I guess I'll just have to accept that I won't get better.

To Alan *on suffering, crying, and despair:*

I'll try to explain my anger, not only to you but also to myself. And I do mean explain, rather than excuse, because I know it's wrong.

I really don't know how I am going to be able to cope with living with FA, especially when I know the progression is likely to continue until I die!

And how will you be able to cope with all that? You already do far too much for me. And I love you so much that I can't bear to see you so tired because of me.

The carers found me crying, but it was only because I was wishing I didn't have my FA, and could grow old gracefully with you, and be able to look after you when you're ill or just tired.

When I wake up crying something you can't understand, it usually means I'm too hot in the summer. I suppose it might mean I'm too cold, but that would be very unusual.

I was so cold last night. If you hadn't cuddled me so closely, I might have panicked earlier. As it was, when you didn't understand me asking you to close the window, you actually opened more windows!

I was terribly angry at myself, both for telling you about my sore legs and for showing any discomfort.

Please, could you straighten my thumbs?

I don't like a big cushion in my back because it makes holding my head up more difficult.

I'm determined not to get upset about the situation. It would only make matters worse.

Another lovely day, but the feeling of not really being there was very strong today! So much so, that I am beginning to worry about this.

You do far too much for me already, and I find it virtually impossible not to get upset. I often wish I still had control over my emotions when things go wrong.

I apologise for blaming you for putting egg in my dinner, when there was none. I guess I'm just losing my ability to taste, which seems terribly unfair, because I've already lost so much. What's next?

I feel so bad today – kind of not really there – and I can't really feel my lips or see clearly or hardly hear anything. I know what the cause is – my FA. You said you wanted to know. ... I've had numb lips for a year, but it's worse now.

I'm so sorry for making all that noise. It must have been awful!

It's so difficult when you can't speak. I'm sorry. I just wanted to tell you how much I enjoyed today.

Jane wrote often and at length on her problems with hearing, speaking, and communication:

I feel so alone at times! I can't hear much and I have hardly any voice! No one makes any special effort to *talk* to me! To use a computer would be one way, or just to sit very near and speak very loudly and clearly! This is not strictly accurate, but it often seems so!

We will need to use our PCs to communicate from now on since you can hardly understand a word I say. For example, when you come in, I usually ask you how your day was and you ask me how mine was, but I bet you never understand the reply.

You must remember how to speak to me? The best way is on the computer, but you can also sit next to me and speak clearly and slowly. Please, could you tell me what's happening in general?

Once a day, please, could you write to me using your laptop? This is essential now. Tell me everything important, please!

The only reason I'm always writing is because no one can be bothered to talk to me in a way I understand. The best way to do this, especially if there's any background noise, is to use the computer. Actually, this is the only way now. For example, you said quite a lot today. Please, could you repeat all you said, using the computer? Johnny is very talkative when he gets home every day, but I'm afraid I often pretend to understand him. I only wish I still could.

I'm sorry for your being married to someone like me! It's not my choice for things to be so hard. I've got very little control over my emotions; hence all the crying. Something new is that my head is full of noise all the time, only it's not what's really going on; it's most often things I've tried to say repeated over and over again by everyone else, even when I know they're not there.

You must be so tired after doing so much! And you, Johnny, didn't you tell me you had a presentation? How did it go? Forgive me if I got that wrong, but my hearing's virtually non-existent!

You must realise that I may have something important to tell you when you get home. I can't rely on my voice any longer.

There's so much I've wanted to say this weekend that it'd take me absolutely ages to type everything. So, as usual, I'll have to start with the essentials.

When you don't understand me, just get out Tobii.

Remember to use your computer to talk to me, because I feel so isolated. Please, could you write the main news for me and tell me what's been going on in the world and with you and Johnny?

Remember to take my writing board everywhere we go, and always take a clear marker.

This morning I became very upset, primarily because of the noise I hear in my head.

My hearing just got dramatically worse, practically overnight. Why?

I can hear voices; I just can't make them out!

My hearing is an absolute nightmare. There's always lots of noise in my head, but most of it has little to do with what's happening at the time.

These days, the noise I hear in my head is almost constant, but right now, I seem to be experiencing a rare moment of silence.

You can't have any idea how frightening it is to be completely deaf and mute. I'm not completely deaf in the normal sense, though. No, it's much worse, because I can hear lots of noise, but it's not what's actually happening. I hear voices, but they're very loud – almost deafening – and completely unrecognisable.

Most of the noise I hear seems to be words and phrases I've tried to say which no one understood. I hear these phrases repeated over and over again very clearly by everyone else, even the television! The rest of what I hear is mainly things I've heard, or think I've heard, but struggled to understand. Again, repeated over and over very clearly by others who are not there! I know what I am hearing is not real, but this doesn't help to take the noise in my head away.

My condition has been getting worse, particularly my hearing and speech. No one can understand most of what I am saying, but quite a few can understand the odd word. This is probably one of the most distressing things to happen so far, as it's so isolating.

I'm not crying because I'm thirsty or anything so stupidly mundane. It's because I don't know if I can cope with the progression of this illness any longer. I went to church this morning to ask for God's help. Sometimes I think you'd be happier with someone you could talk to.

My hearing and my speech are both very bad today. I can hardly hear or say anything, especially when there is any background noise, as in church.

My speech started to disappear when my hearing got really bad. They seem to be connected, so I'm hoping that if you can help my hearing, then my speech will come back.

My voice is connected with my hearing, so I hope the doctors can improve my hearing.

My hearing is considerably worse, and I've lost any voice I had almost completely. These must be connected, as they happened at the same time. This is one of the most distressing things ever to happen, as it's so isolating!

I'm looking forward to going to London and having my hearing improved. That should also improve my speech.

You wanted me to tell you, Doctor, more about my condition at the moment. The worst thing is still my hearing and my lack of speech. I can hear lots of noise in my head, but most of it doesn't mean anything. The only people I can understand are those who sit very close to me and speak loudly – without shouting – and clearly and slowly. A lot of the noise I hear comes from the few words I hear, repeated over and over again, probably most of it comprising things I've tried to say.

Please, could you tell me *everything* the doctor said?

What a lovely day, but I feel as though I'm not really there.

Another lovely day, but the feeling of not really being there was very strong today!

I wish there was a treatment for FA. Then I'd have some hope.

You asked me if there was anyone I wanted you to pray for. I was answering you. I get so upset when you can't even understand me when I answer a question.

I'm sorry if I worried you. I guess I must've had a bad day. I must've been very tired. I couldn't hold my head up properly.

That was a lovely day. I hope you enjoyed it too? I'm very tired, though! Can I go to bed early? Not necessarily to sleep. Maybe we could just watch TV in bed? Can I take Tobii out with me tomorrow?

Please, could you record the live final of *Britain's Got Talent* in the bedroom tomorrow evening?

The time has come to ask Helen for a breath control for Tobii. Like Stephen Hawking. Do you think Gramps would like large-print books?

I must be getting worse, because I can no longer hear everything Angie says, whereas I always could before! I loved hearing about the little dog, Boxer! You probably know all about him!

Your guitar sounds lovely.

As for Tobii, I will use him when we go out, but with the new chin switch. Only turn it on, though, when you want to understand me, or else I'll be a performing animal again!

I feel sorry for you, being stuck with someone like me, especially since I lost any voice I ever had. If I could speak, I'd have told you to cancel the carers today, so we could have a long lie.

I'm not trying to sound so pathetic or so loud. … When I try to speak, it just comes out like that. I have absolutely no control over how it sounds any more. I can't control the tone.

I think that I'll be well enough to go to church tomorrow, but remember I can't hear anything in that hall, not even everything that you or Betty say, so I'll definitely need my board and a willing scribe.

I'm so sorry if I seemed angry with you, but I am losing so much now that it often seems like a waking nightmare!

I'm sorry about the noise last night. I think it was just a nightmare. Is Johnny OK?

Last night, I had a waking nightmare. It was so real, just like now. In my nightmare, I wasn't able to communicate with you at all because I couldn't use my Tobii.

What a lovely day! But what was everyone saying, because I couldn't hear a word?

Will you tell me what everyone was saying?

I can hear everyone's voices. I just can't make out what they're saying!

JANE Another lovely day! What was that song you were singing with the taxi driver? It must be very popular, because I've heard you singing it with Johnny, Angie, Zoe, and others. When I say "hear", I don't mean any words, only a familiar noise.

ALAN Sorry, darling, no one was singing. Your hearing is being muddled by the illness.

JANE Why won't you tell me the words of that song you keep singing with everyone? It must be quite popular. I've heard you singing it with Johnny and with the carers, and with the taxi drivers.

ALAN So sorry, sweetheart, there really is no singing. I don't burst into song with random taxi drivers. This is not *The Sound of Music*. What you describe sounds more serious than normal deafness. It must be a neurological symptom.

JANE Why won't you tell me the words of that song you keep singing with everyone? What's the big deal?

ALAN Sorry, darling, it must be your hearing playing tricks on you, when you hear conversations but can't make out the words.

Travel

On cruises

*W*e're going on another cruise in just over a week. I thought I wouldn't be well enough to go. Just shows you that there's life in the old dog yet!

I'm really looking forward to our cruise! Cruises are so liberating for disabled people. They can actually enjoy a full holiday at last! Everything is in the same place! Where else could a disabled person experience in comfort a holiday with the latest entertainment, fine dining, and many interesting and often exotic places all over the world to visit?

Another important consideration for me, personally, is that my beloved long-suffering husband, who always looks after me, has other passengers he can talk to, as my voice is now virtually impossible to understand.

A cruise also caters for all kinds of disability, from people with diabetes to people like me, who have to be fed and have their food pureed. No wonder I'm looking forward to our cruise!

Can we afford to go on holiday? A cruise would be the easiest to organise, as you only have to order the hoist and commode. They're used to all kinds of disability. Our anniversary is jade/coral. I'd love a coral necklace!

Do you think P&O still have places on their Norwegian cruise?

On Friday, could you take me to Eltham for the whole day, leaving as though we were going to church? We need so many summer things for the cruise, you as well as me. You could take me to Total Beauty and we could have lunch at the coffee shop where you get steak.

For our anniversary next Saturday, it would be lovely to have a new camera, especially with the cruise coming up. We could give it to each other as an anniversary present.

What would you like to do tomorrow? I'd like you to buy yourself some summer clothes for the cruise.

Remember what the taxi driver said about the temperature in Istanbul now. You will need summer clothes.

We've got everything for the cruise, except I really want a white summer skirt, as well as a suitcase to fit inside the others.

I'm sure the places where we will be staying could hire us a mobile hoist and have it waiting in our room.

I'll have to get some soft shoes for this cruise. One black pair, one blue pair.

Could you read me what it says about our cruise in the big P&O brochure?

Could you help me with lists on Sunday for the cruise?

It's a pity that we can't have our new memory-foam mattress on the cruise, because it's so comfortable.

I'm really looking forward to the cruise, but I'm not much company now. Will you be all right with only me to talk to?

I'd like to find out more about the cruise, particularly a map of the ship.

The cruise is only four weeks away tomorrow! I've got to lose weight. I know that's virtually impossible for someone like me, but I've got to try!

It's a twenty-three-night cruise, so there'll be ample opportunity to put on weight! I'm really looking forward to this cruise, so I've already started the diet.

I'm worried about the cruise. I really won't be able to eat much, not even all the dinner, even if I have no lunch.

Could you ask our waiter to give me small portions to ensure I don't gain too much weight?

Yesterday, I noticed that you've put on weight! It doesn't suit you. You look older! I know I can't talk, but you're lucky in that you can lose weight quickly. You look so young when you're slim.

Could you read me the cruise itinerary and descriptions of everywhere we stop? I would also like to see a deck plan of the ship and to know whether the rooms are air-conditioned and what the mattresses are made of.

Is Zoe coming tomorrow? If so, could you put your cotton shirts on the table, as well as the ironing from my wardrobe? I could go to that beauty parlour in Eltham before the cruise.

You've two or three cotton shirts which should be ironed. Also, I've several wrap-around skirts in my wardrobe that need lengthening. Have you got anything else for the cruise needing mending?

Remember to leave some sewing and/or ironing on the table for Zoe to take home. It's quite urgent!

Let's try to get everything we need for the holiday in Southend, including something for Sophie and some more wrinkle cream for me.

Did the podiatrist say anything about me wearing shoes instead of the diabetic slippers? The reason I'm asking is because it would be easier for us on our excursions in Russia.

Please, could Zoe dye my eyelashes and eyebrows today, and again just before the cruise?

I should see my doctor before the cruise, like last year when I actually had two courses of antibiotics before we left. We also took two small bottles of antibiotics in our case for my own use, one of which you mixed up for me with water in Malta after a thunderstorm.

Would you like Zoe to paint my nails a brighter shade of pink?

Remember to show me a deck plan of the *Arcadia* and find out if the rooms are air-conditioned and what the mattresses are made of.

Last time we were in Helsinki, we took boat rides all round Helsinki

Bay. We also took the ferry from Helsinki to Tallinn, in Estonia. It was wonderful! I can't wait to go there again on our Baltic cruise.

On board (at last):

You've done everything very well! What time's dinner, and where is it? What's the dress code? Will you read me today's ship magazine?

Jade wedding anniversary cruise, November–December 2012 (twenty-three nights)

(Jane's newsletter, 28 December 2012)

In 2012, to celebrate their thirty-fifth wedding anniversary – coral and jade – almost a year early, Jane and Alan sailed to the Eastern Mediterranean. The cruise was to include wheelchair excursions to Galilee, Nazareth, Bethlehem, and Jerusalem.

Jane wrote as follows:

Hi,

Alan and I have just returned from a truly wonderful pre-Christmas cruise of the Eastern Mediterranean with P&O. We visited many exotic and interesting places, and everywhere the people were delightful, from local wheelchair-cab drivers in Limassol to friendly street traders in Istanbul.

We were impressed by how truly ancient some places are, such as Rhodes, the oldest inhabited medieval city in Europe, and Ephesus, where we visited the Basilica of John the Apostle, as well as the house where Mary, the mother of Jesus, is believed to have lived in the years following the Crucifixion.

Jane and Alan at Mary's House (Ephesus, 2012)

Our holiday began disastrously when Alan was informed, when checking in on the boat, that on account of the recent hostilities (and in spite of the ceasefire), P&O would not be calling at Israel, so we would not be able after all to go on our excursions to Nazareth and Galilee, nor to Bethlehem or Jerusalem. We were both devastated.

On reflection, though, I can see that they would have had in mind the safety of passengers and crew. In fact, P&O had earlier in the year cancelled their planned visit to Alexandria in Egypt for the same reason.

Never one to hide my emotions, I promptly burst into tears. Alan was given the option of cancellation (though with no promise of our money back), but neither of us could bear the idea of losing our long-awaited holiday entirely, so we agreed, somewhat reluctantly, to go on the cruise. P&O staff took us into a small side room and assured me that we could go to Israel another time (though no one said when or how) and that we would still be going to lots of interesting places.

Once we had recovered from the initial shock, we were able to start to look forward to the rest of the cruise. We would be going to Cyprus and spending longer in both Istanbul and Malta. Although it didn't make up for seeing the land where Jesus lived in human form, the places we visited did certainly inspire the imagination.

Around 5 p.m. we went to find our restaurant, and as usual on cruise holidays, we were directed to the restaurant farthest away from our cabin! There, we were allocated a large corner table to ourselves by a very nice head waiter, who looked after us well.

The chef blended all my food and made all my desserts diabetic. The food itself was superb, very nearly Michelin-class! We were very tired after dinner, so we went back to our cabin and finished unpacking.

The next day we took the opportunity to explore the ship. The *Aurora* is a very stylish ship with a kind of old-fashioned air. There were quite a few luxury shops on board, and by way of complete surprise, Alan bought me my new jade wedding anniversary ring one day from the posh jeweller's on the ship! It's a lovely ring. Although it was ridiculously expensive, I do feel as though we were meant to go on this cruise and buy this ring because we've been through so much in the past two years.

The weather in Vigo and Lisbon was cloudy and wet, although quite warm. However, since we'd already visited them both on a previous cruise, in the brilliant sunshine, we weren't too bothered by the weather and just went shopping. When we arrived in Lisbon, the ship docked exactly at the point where our balcony was level with the Portuguese replica of the famous *Christ the King* statue in Brazil, which was reassuring! In Lisbon we were able to buy some excellent cream for the eczema which I had developed on hearing that we wouldn't be going to Israel.

Jesus seemed to be reminding us that although the misunderstandings of humankind had made our visit to His homeland impossible, He was always with us. We would later visit Ephesus, where His disciple John is believed to have pastored the local church and looked after Jesus's mother, Mary, in the years following the Crucifixion.

Then we had three days at sea. We had always enjoyed these days best on previous cruises, and it was the same on this cruise. You could relax in an atmosphere of sheer luxury. The free self-service restaurant on deck 12 served a leisurely breakfast until 11 a.m., and then you could sunbathe, swim in one of three pools (one indoor), and go to the spa (beauty parlour and hairdresser), as I did the first Tuesday and then every week, or the indoor gym. The list is endless. And when you add the daily six-course gourmet dinner and the nightly entertainment (shows, singers, musicians, and dancers), you can easily see why we appreciated the days at sea!

When we arrived in Athens it was, unfortunately, rather cloudy. This somewhat marred our first view of the Acropolis.

I thought Athens quite an ugly city, to be honest, despite glimpses of past glory. We spent most of our time in an archaeological museum with an impressive range of truly ancient statues and exhibits, including endless examples of fine figures of the male form throughout classical antiquity (!), as well as the famous Mask of Agamemnon (reputed brother-in-law of Helen of Troy), dated around 1500 BC.

Highlights of our holiday were many and included the following:

In Istanbul we picnicked by the Spice Bazaar; befriended the local wildlife; visited the Blue Mosque and the Hagia Sophia; watched Turkish carpets being made; haggled for trinkets in the Grand Bazaar; and marvelled at the beauty of the city at night.

In Cyprus we met Santa Claus in the blazing sunshine and were driven around town by Lazarus (yes, honestly!), who spoke no English and resembled Manuel from *Fawlty Towers*. He turned out to drive what appeared to be the only wheelchair cab in Limassol!

In Rhodes we explored the fourteenth-century Palace of the Grand Master of the Knights of Rhodes, admired the unsurpassed beauty of the town itself (in some ways reminiscent of Tallinn), and made a mental note to come back soon.

In Malta we left behind a storm at sea, to be greeted by a hailstorm as we made our way up the (very) steep hill from the docks to the Old Town on our first day in Valetta. Fortunately, the weather was superb on our second day and we were able to enjoy some truly wonderful views of the island and a panoramic sweep of the Grand Harbour below.

In short, we had the holiday of a lifetime – not perhaps the holiday we had expected or dreamed of, as we were unable to visit the Holy Land, but a wonderful break nevertheless. We had the chance to get a proper rest in luxurious surroundings and to see some of the most beautiful and amazing places in the world, mostly in very good weather.

We are sorry this is now too late to qualify as a Christmas newsletter, so instead would like to take the opportunity to say a very big "Happy New Year" to you all!

With lots of love,
Jane

Coral wedding anniversary cruise

(Jane's newsletter, November 2013)

Jane and Alan had enjoyed themselves so much on their cruise back in 2012 that they decided to have another cruise the following year, in August–September 2013, to celebrate the same anniversary (thirty-fifth) all over again, calling it coral this time, instead of jade! Jane wrote as follows:

Hi,

Our recent Baltic cruise was wonderful. I was able to take with me my Tobii communications device, which I now use to help me write and "talk". This was wonderful. I was even able to start this newsletter on the cruise, on our luxury balcony!

Jane busy writing at sea on her Baltic cruise

Alan and I were able to celebrate the actual day of our thirty-fifth wedding anniversary in style, with balloons above our dinner table, serenaded by our waiters, who sang "Congratulations" and presented us with a delicious coral anniversary cake to take to our cabin!

Alan and Jane, dining in style at sea on the day of
their thirty-fifth wedding anniversary

We visited seven very interesting and different countries. From Kristiansand, the most southerly town in Norway, where we were given a guided tour of the neo-Gothic cathedral (Domkirke), completed in 1885, we travelled to Copenhagen in Denmark, with its famous *Little Mermaid* statue to welcome you, and its wide, busy, colourful main shopping area bordering the canal, with every kind of stall. Then we went on to the fascinating German seaside town of Warnemunde, where the locals were hosting an organic food and drink festival. Alan brought me a delicious organic peach juice, while he had his usual fat German sausage. Typical!

Then came Tallinn, in Estonia. We had been there before, but we discovered more delightfully quaint places in the old town, including the old market square, which was built round an old church. We also found a café where they both roasted their own coffee beans and made their own chocolate, which of course we had to sample!

Next came St Petersburg in Russia, which was our favourite port! According to our young Russian guide, St Petersburg only has fifty to sixty days of sunshine a year, and we got two of the very best, warm and dry, perfect to show off the beauty and majesty of old Russia! First we visited the Hermitage, one of the largest and oldest museums in the world, part of which is housed in the Winter Palace, a former residence of the tsars. The Hermitage was founded in 1764 by Catherine the Great and has been open to the public since 1852. It boasts one of the finest art collections in the world! The old masters alone are phenomenal. I had seen Michelangelo's *La Pieta* in St Peter's in Rome (back in 1977), and in the Hermitage we saw Leonardo's *Benois Madonna* (or *Madonna and Child with Flowers*), which for centuries had been considered lost. We were taken to the exact room where the Russian Revolution of February 1917 began, with the clocks remaining frozen at 12:10 p.m., the precise time when Nicholas II was forced to abdicate and the Romanov dynasty was replaced by a provisional revolutionary government. The following day we visited Peterhof, the summer palace of Peter the Great, and its magnificent gardens, the week before the G20 met there. It really was spectacular. The lovely gardens were filled with equally spectacular waterfalls and fountains. Later we sampled a typical Russian meal, in the splendour of the palace's own restaurant, the part I enjoyed most being the sparkling wine!

We had been to Helsinki before, but soon discovered new gems, including a lovely little park, where we found the most delicious Finnish ice cream and a lovely chai latte! The last time we had been there, our hotel was next to the fish market by the harbour. We had gone on boat rides around the islands surrounding Helsinki most days, as well as on a day trip with the locals by ferry to Tallinn. This time, although we found the fish market, there was no time for boat rides.

Our last stop was at the Swedish capital of Stockholm. This was the only place where it actually rained. Fortunately, we were in the Old Town (or Gamla Stan) at the time, a glorious labyrinth of charming cobbled streets, alleyways, townhouses, and meeting squares, so we were able to pop into an interesting shop or two until the worst was over. This area reminded me of the Lanes in Brighton, but on a grander scale.

The last three days of our cruise were spent at sea, which is always the best of all for us, because they are the most relaxing. After breakfast on the day of our anniversary, a church service was held in the theatre of the ship, led by the captain, a formidable but jovial woman who delivered an amusing sermon and even cracked a few jokes. After dinner, we saw a West End standard production of *The Songs of Freddie Mercury*, and retired to the bar for Bailey's before bed.

All in all, it was another wonderful holiday. We were so grateful for the opportunity to celebrate our anniversary in such style.

With lots of love,
Jane

APPENDICES

1. Interview with Local NHS Trust Magazine, 2014

2. Jane's Early Years, as Remembered by Her Brother and Sisters

3. Alan's Recollection of Jane's Later Years: "The Wonder of You"

Interview with Local NHS Trust Magazine, 2014

This interview formed the basis of a feature article that appeared in the Spring 2014 (Issue 34) edition of Oxleas Exchange, *the magazine of the Oxleas NHS Foundation Trust. It sheds light on how the book came about and what Jane was going through at the time.*

JANE I am 58 years old. Alan and I have been married for over thirty-five years, and we have a grown-up son of 33. We met at university in Scotland, where I was studying psychology. At university I used to be able to type my essays, very slowly, with an early electric typewriter. I had to dictate my exams to a postgraduate "scribe" as, even back then in the 1970s, such was the nature of my disability that I would have been unable to type fast enough to keep up.

SPEECH THERAPIST What condition led to your current state of health, and when did this happen?

JANE I was diagnosed with Friedreich's ataxia, a progressive neurological disorder, in 1969, at the age of 13. I was told I would gradually get worse, would never walk again, would soon be in a wheelchair, and may only have three years to live. Forty-five years later, however, I am still here, though my entire condition – including speech, hearing, movement, and eyesight – has been slowly deteriorating over the years, with everything slowly becoming more difficult as each day passes. For instance, I no longer listen to radio or watch TV, as I can't hear what anyone is saying and the subtitles are too fast to keep up with and too small to see. I can't hear what anyone says unless they sit very close to me, one at a time, and speak very slowly. If there is any background noise, I hear nothing at all.

In 2011 I nearly died as a result of a serious chest infection. I was put under palliative care and was nursed from home. I had a morphine pump. Alan was told by the doctor to let close family know I may not have long to live and therefore if they wanted to see me again they ought to come soon, as otherwise I may no longer be alive! Needless to say, I survived that illness and was in time allowed to leave my bed and gradually get back to a more normal life in my new tilt-and-recline wheelchair, which I now needed owing to weakening of my muscles and general strength. I was diagnosed with dysphagia, as my swallowing has deteriorated. I now need to have all of my drinks thickened and all of my food blended, to prevent aspiration.

Jane, Mary, Ann, and John (2011)

The following year, 2012, I was suddenly taken extremely ill once again, and this time hospitalised with diabetic ketoacidosis (DKA) and extreme dehydration. DKA is a serious complication of diabetes that occurs when the patient's body, unable to produce enough insulin, produces high levels of blood acids called ketones. I was diagnosed with type 1 diabetes, which I later found out is a common occurrence in late-stage Friedreich's ataxia. I was terribly ill. Alan was told by the hospital that if I went into heart failure, they would not treat me, as my body was too weak to survive. I was unable to hear what anyone said while in hospital, and no one could understand me at all. I didn't even know where I was and thought I had been kidnapped. In time, amazingly, I beat the odds and recovered enough to be sent home. Soon afterwards, Alan took me on a cruise to celebrate our anniversary!

SPEECH THERAPIST How do you use the equipment?

JANE I use my Tobii all day, every day, with the communication software Grid 2, and this now provides me with the voice I had lost. I use it to "speak" to people who I have not been able to talk with for many years. Very few people can understand me now, as my own speech has become increasingly less distinct. My own father, who is 86, whom we have lunch with every week, often at our local Italian restaurant, was amazed when he heard my new "voice" for the first time. He could not figure out how I was speaking when he couldn't see my lips move! I took my Tobii with us on our most recent cruise, visiting Norway, Sweden, Finland, Russia, Estonia, Germany, and Denmark. This allowed me to relay to Alan what I wanted to do each day, as well as my thoughts and reflections on the holiday and the wonderful places we were visiting. I am now able to take Tobii with me to our local church, where I have many friends. I was able to use Tobii to say "Merry Christmas and a happy New Year" to all my friends when we had house church a few days before Christmas.

SPEECH THERAPIST What do you use Tobii for most?

JANE Most of all I am using Tobii to write my own memoirs, *Forever Yours*, which is an autobiography, written in the third person, based on my own life story. I have got up to the year 1980 so far (from

1955). Alan and I hope one day to publish the book. I also use Tobii every day to "speak" to Alan, even when he is at work, by writing out in full sentences the essence of what I would otherwise want to say if I could still speak normally. When he gets home, I press Speak and the Tobii reads everything I have been writing with a voice very similar to the voice I once had. Alan saves everything I write so we don't lose it and emails any messages to him from me to his mobile phone so that he can refer to what I have asked him or been telling him, or what has been worrying me. For instance, I like to say where I want to go on a Friday when he takes me out – which shops I want to go to and what we need to get. I write lists to let him know what we are to do. I also write lists for my carers to tell them what I would like them to do. This way I can request such things as a head massage, something special for dinner, or to have my hair or nails done. This is wonderful, because I now have a sense of being involved in making the decisions that affect my own life and I can contribute ideas and suggestions.

SPEECH THERAPIST What was life like for you before this happened?

JANE The worst thing of all in recent years has been the devastating loss of my ability to speak, see, and hear properly. This has been a gradual process, but with a noticeably marked and sharp deterioration of my ability to engage as I used to with the world around me in the past few years. Now it is virtually impossible for me to have any kind of conversation with anyone at all without the Tobii, not even Alan (who had, until around mid-2013, always been able to understand me). Before I was loaned Tobii and the Grid 2, I was in complete despair. My health was getting worse in a devastating way and I had lost any sense of involvement in my own life. I felt so isolated. I was very depressed much of the time and felt alienated from my environment – a patient, not a person.

SPEECH THERAPIST How have the speech therapists helped you?

JANE You and your team have saved my life and given me back something to live for by arranging for me to have the equipment and head-switch mechanism that allows me to communicate again. I still find life terribly hard and things are far from easy, but the Tobii makes it possible for me to keep trying and never give up. You even managed to get me a special trolley on wheels for my Tobii so that I can use it in bed. This has been invaluable on a number of occasions when I have been unwell recently and had to go to bed early or was not well enough to get up. Alan was able to set the Tobii up for me in bed to allow me to continue where I had left off.

SPEECH THERAPIST What is the thing that sustains you most?

JANE Being able to keep in contact with friends and family, by using the Tobii voice and by receiving and sending emails, has proved invaluable in giving me continued hope in spite of the obvious problems Alan and I face on a daily basis. My faith in Jesus, however, sustains me most of all, as I know He has a plan for my future, even though I may not be able to see this or understand it right now.

SPEECH THERAPIST How has having the equipment changed the way you view the future?

JANE I am now far more positive about the future and look forward to meeting my friends and family, because I can have something to say. And of course I am looking forward to having my book published … and our next cruise!

Jane's Early Years, as Remembered by Her Brother and Sisters

Although Jane has been without doubt the single most important influence on each of our lives, we were pretty much a normal bunch of children with our own rivalries and resentments, jostling for the attention of our parents. The fact that Jane was disabled and that her disability appeared to worsen over time was our normality. Being a few years younger than she was, none of us can actually remember a time when Jane was not, to some extent, disabled.

We remember her in callipers after measles trying to cross the room unaided. We remember her secondary school ensuring that all her lessons were on the ground floor, though chemistry was banned as she was considered too unsteady for the practicals (thereby effectively stymieing her ambition to be a doctor). We remember her clinging on to her closest friend, F (Christine Cutbush), to get around – a likely pairing, both then overweight and not well, though fiercely intelligent.

Jane was spoilt something rotten by her mother; nothing was ever too much for "poor Jane", with Jane nothing but rude to the old "Moo" in return. She was also a bully, if not always to us, then certainly at school. Nothing too unusual here, perhaps – well within the remit of an eldest sibling who was not quite the same as other children.

The diagnosis, when it came, was not an earth-shattering event. Only Mary remembers visiting Jane at the National Hospital at the time. When told by our parents – not immediately and together, but over time and separately, in apparent justification of some favour that Jane had been shown – that Jane had only a few years to live, it seemed entirely plausible and offered hope of a more normal existence thereafter.

Our parents, understandably, doted on Jane. Everything had to be altered for her. From days out and holidays to the entire back end of the house at South Close, all plans were made around her. In her later teens, she was allowed to get drunk, a pleasure denied her siblings. We were not even allowed to argue with her, in case we upset her. Indeed, our parents made every attempt to make life not just as normal as possible for her but also as easy as possible, regardless of the impact that this might have on their other children.

Despite our sense of normality, as teenagers we were all hugely embarrassed by Jane's condition. Boyfriends were not brought home; wheelchairs were hidden from public view. We also all resented, to a lesser or greater extent, the care and attention that was lavished on Jane by our parents, but not – as we would have it – on us.

But we were not uncaring, often taking Jane out, be it around the local park or to the Silver Lounge, and writing up the school essays she dictated, and doing the same under exam conditions in her actual O and A levels. Mary remembers teaching Jane to drive. The family car had been especially adapted in some forlorn hope that perhaps Jane would maintain sufficient control of her upper body, if not her legs, for long enough at least to make it worthwhile. Our mother was too scared to get into a car with Jane driving. Mary also sewed Jane's wedding dress over the wheels of her wheelchair, as if this would somehow give the impression of her walking down the aisle. We even, when a little older, connived with our parents in the free rein that Jane was given, going out in the evenings when Jane was hosting a party, only to find the washing machine full of beer on our return.

Yet at the same time there are certain memories that stand out and suggest that Jane was not as accepting of or as matter-of-fact about her condition, as her memoir might suggest, the incessant screams of "Why me?!" being one. The screaming could go on for hours, filling the entire house, and still haunting to this day. Jane's utter contempt for and venomous hatred of God and anything religious is another example, to the extent that her Christian faith in the final years of her life is, frankly, at least to her siblings, utterly unbelievable. "I hate vicars" was not only her most commonly voiced sentiment; it seemed also to be the credo by which she lived her life.

Jane never spoke directly about her condition. Her actions suggested to us that she didn't accept it and fought it violently, yet she wouldn't have anything to do with it. Her illness was like an unwelcome guest at the dinner table, spoken to occasionally, formalities observed but largely ignored, only to be railed at relentlessly afterwards.

John, Mary, and Ann
(Jane's brother and sisters)

Alan's Recollection of Jane's Later Years: "The Wonder of You"

Jane's life was a story of facing adversity head-on and carrying on regardless. Never giving up. Never even considering giving up. Staring it down. With her smile intact. There's so much I could say about Jane, but none of it would be good enough. None of it would do her justice. She was quite simply the most wonderful, the most beautiful, the most incredible person I will ever meet. I am so privileged to have had the opportunity to share my life with her.

Losing the ability to walk, Jane negotiated the corridors of her girls' grammar school first with a walking frame, later with a wheelchair. Increasingly unsteady on her feet, she took up horse riding as a hobby, encouraged by her parents to be confident and fearless.

Jane on horseback (1970)

Having lost the ability to write fast enough to keep up, she dictated her exams to a scribe, often a family member, earning a rare A in A-level history, specialising in a period that was to become a lifelong passion – the Tudors. Jane wrote her essays at school, and later at university, with an early electric typewriter. She had just enough strength to pick out the characters one finger at a time. It took an age. But she never complained or gave up. Once, Jane borrowed a friend's lecture notes for a sociology course she had found too dull to attend. Jane memorised the notes the night before the exam, only to be awarded a higher grade for the paper than the friend who had lent her his notes. Once at university, faced with a friend who challenged her not to overindulge in Mars Bars, since to eat too many could be fatal for someone in her supposedly frail condition, she ate six Mars Bars in a row, just to prove him wrong, and lived to tell the tale.

Jane and I met at Stirling University in 1976. By that time she was unable to stand or walk at all. In our almost forty years together, I never saw Jane stand up. She was, and is, and always will be the love of my life. After university, in 1980, Jane and I, with baby Johnny in tow, made the trip south to settle in Eltham, south-east London, where I had been offered a place at a teacher training college. Jane's parents had moved that year from Bexleyheath to live in Eltham, so there was no shortage of willing help available with baby Johnny while he was small. Jane and I missed Scotland very much, but we soon settled in. Jane considered herself a Londoner more than anything, so she was glad to have the opportunity to show me around her favourite city at our leisure.

Alan, Jane, and Johnny (Eltham, 1981)

Jane and I loved going to the theatre, the cinema, the ballet, the museums, and the art galleries in London together. It was exciting to be part of such a metropolitan city, with so much going on. Jane's favourite ballet was *Swan Lake*. The sheer beauty of the score and the tragedy of the story would move Jane to tears of joy. She told me she could often see herself in dreams dancing like Margot Fonteyn with a young Rudolf Nureyev. She would wake to find herself increasingly unable to move, but in her dreams there were no such limitations.

Throughout the 1980s and '90s, Jane had her hair styled at Vidal Sassoon, South Molton Street, near Oxford Street. We went to a number of concerts to see some of her favourite artists, including Elton John (twice), Paul McCartney, and Rod Stewart, not to mention Elvis

Presley (or at least a hologram of the great man on stage at the Wembley Arena). Jane loved musicals. We went to see quite a few in the West End, everything from *Mary Poppins* to *Dirty Dancing*. Our tastes were far from highbrow, but we felt no pressing need to pretend otherwise. To cope with a condition such as Jane's, it is essential to live a life as close to normal as possible and never to limit the opportunities for light relief.

Up until the early 2000s, Jane's hearing was reasonable, so she could still follow TV, something she did later on with the help of subtitles. We developed similar tastes, as we enjoyed watching films and TV together rather than alone. Jane loved comedies with ludicrous exaggerated characters, such as *Young Frankenstein*, *Fawlty Towers*, *The Fall and Rise of Reginald Perrin*, and *'Allo 'Allo!* We attended the Henley Royal Regatta most years with Jane's dad, Peter, who had rowed for his university back in medical school days in New Zealand, though Jane seemed to prefer the Pimm's to the rowing!

Jane with her dad, Peter, at the Henley Royal Regatta (July 2005)

Until around 2005, Jane could still really enjoy music. She had her own playlist of around two hundred songs, all selected by Jane herself, which she would listen to on random shuffle via the DVD player on our TV. Jane loved having time on her own, just to read, watch movies, or relax. She particularly disliked the idea of being "looked after" all the time.

Jane enjoyed inventing recipes to surprise us with later. She would recite, to me or to her carer Zoe, the ingredients for a meal she had just thought up in her head, and would describe precisely how the dish was to be prepared and cooked. Jane was creative and loved to take a lead. I always thought of Jane as a natural alpha female.

If Jane had been less disabled, she would without doubt have been the driver in the family. I, on the other hand, was always a nervous driver. Jane used to direct me when we were out. I famously have no sense of direction. This worked well until Jane began to lose her voice, in the mid-nineties, which would leave me hanging at junctions with no idea which way to turn. Thankfully, buses with wheelchair ramps began appearing on the streets of London in the years that followed.

Jane and I visited many countries. She was famous for her love of cruises. Even when her food had to be blended and spoon-fed, and her drinks thickened and given through a straw, we still went on cruises, and Jane would still send dishes back to the kitchen if they failed to impress, much to my embarrassment. Even when Jane's wheelchair, nearer the end, was as long as a bed, we still went on buses, trains, boats, and by taxi.

Jane used to live for her holidays more than anything. We had lovely holidays all over the world. Favourite destinations included New York, where we visited Johnny in 2000, while he was at drama school; our romantic silver wedding anniversary cruise of the Norwegian fjords; a majestic cruise to Madeira and the Canary Islands to celebrate our pearl wedding anniversary; Rheinsberg, in Germany, where we sipped champagne at an outdoor opera, surrounded by fairy-tale castles, and were taken white-water rafting by a guide who Jane thought looked like Johnny Depp; Helsinki, where we cruised around the bay on tour boats most days and feasted each morning on an abundance of fresh salmon; Tallinn, where we experienced a tantalising blend of the modern and the medieval; Prague, where we dined in the Grand Hotel Europa, on

Wenceslas Square, in the opulent dining room on which the actual restaurant aboard the *Titanic* was modelled; Port Grimaud, near St Tropez, where we stayed in a posh wheelchair-accessible caravan close to the beach; and Grado, near Venice, one of nature's hidden gems, where we were mistaken for Germans and were locked for over an hour in the disabled toilet by a befuddled innkeeper with a wartime grudge, nearly missing our flight home.

Jane enjoying the sunshine in Grado (2012)

Other memorable holidays included visits to Vienna, Salzburg, Geneva, Zurich, Oberammergau, Amsterdam, Bruges, Lake Lucerne, Antwerp, and Paris (on many occasions), the last of which was our honeymoon destination back in 1978.

Jane and Alan – Paris honeymoon (1978)

Jane lost the ability to hold a cup, dress, wash and feed herself, put on make-up, and so on, very gradually, during the 1980s and '90s, and in a way, the painstakingly slow nature of the deterioration, over long timescales, made each successive loss all the more devastating. As far back as the early 1980s, Jane had found she was no longer able to use an electric typewriter, as she had as an undergraduate for essays and correspondence. She effectively stopped writing altogether after university, until 2011, and blamed this on the progression of her ataxia. When she did want to write, she would dictate to me what she wanted to say. Jane just got on with things. She refused to pity herself or to be pitied by others.

She typically gave the impression that she was happy deep down and that there was far too much to do to waste time worrying. When things did get too much for her, the anger and frustration would blow up and boil over in the heat of the moment, but any row was soon forgotten. As a rule, Jane lived very deliberately as if nothing was amiss. For many years, I found it difficult to comfort Jane when she was upset. It seemed to me that her frustration was too severe and overwhelming for her to face head-on in the course of day-to-day life. She appeared to choose understandably to bury the anguish deep within. Jane would explain to me that she had to live this way to remain strong.

Jane could throughout the 1980s and '90s still speak fairly clearly, though her speech was slurred. Her hearing was affected by background noise, but generally until the early 2000s, Jane could still make out what people were saying if they sat close to her and spoke clearly and at eye level in a quiet room. Jane grew close to her carers, particularly Zoe, over the years. Jane's listening ear was greatly valued on occasion. She was known and loved for her discretion, compassion, and good advice. As time went on, however, it became more and more difficult for Jane to hear what others were saying. Friends would chat away, enjoying each other's company, assuming Jane was part of the conversation. Later she would ask me what they had all said. I learned to "translate" to make sure she was not left out.

Jane loved reading. She liked hardback books because they were easier to hold. Eventually, around 1998, Jane could no longer turn the pages. This was devastating, as reading was her release, her escape route of choice. The day came, around 2000, when she was no longer able even to hold hardback books. A number of years then passed when Jane was unable to read independently. She could not get to grips with audiobooks or books for the blind. Her hearing had become jumbled (rather like auditory dyslexia) and she could not follow the narrative that way.

When Kindle e-books came in, Jane was an early adopter. We worked out how to use plug-in software intended for the blind to scroll her e-books on a large PC monitor at the slowest and most comfortable speed and in the largest possible font. If anyone sent Jane a message, such as an email or a letter, I would turn it into a massive-font pdf and scroll it for Jane at the slowest speed to allow her to read it. This approach allowed her to continue to enjoy reading independently until very close to the end of her life, even though she could by then no longer turn the pages by hand or by switch.

As time passed, Jane lost virtually all speech and experienced a distressing form of deafness characterised by the gradual loss over time of the ability to follow conversation and be fully part of what was going on. She had to have all of her food blended and her drinks thickened, because of increasing swallowing difficulties.

In anguish and despair, I cried out to the God I had placed my trust in as a child, asking Him to help me and my family with this impossible situation. I knew that I simply could not cope under my own steam any longer. God met with me in a very real and powerful way in 2007 and revealed Himself to me as a loving Father who cared deeply for me and for my family. The Lord Jesus gave me the strength I needed for the final nine years of Jane's life. God filled me with the strength, the love, and the resolve to do everything that needed to be done to make sure Jane's life continued to have meaning and joy to the end, no matter what. I came to know and to experience a love not of my own making: the unconditional love of God, poured out on my heart and on my family. Whereas before I had struggled for so long to cope, as things got steadily worse, turning at one point to the bottle for solace, only to find this a trapdoor to hell itself, at long last I now found I had the strength to carry on.

At first, Jane was horrified. She protested loudly and vociferously and said she wanted a divorce and that she would walk out the door there and then and never return if only she could stand up, if only she were not stuck in her wheelchair, reliant on others for everything. I continued in prayer for Jane to come to faith. Very soon, a growing circle of Christians from all over the world were praying for Jane: for her to be healed, but more importantly for her to come to know the love and mercy of God.

Over the years, as Jane's condition progressed, a number of hospitals, including the National Hospital for Neurology and Neurosurgery; the Queen Elizabeth Hospital, in Woolwich; and Guy's Hospital, helped Jane with a range of medical problems. Jane received excellent care and support throughout. She was at one point included in medical trials aimed at finding a suitable treatment for Friedreich's ataxia. Jane simply loved being included in such trials. It thrilled her to be part of the effort to find a treatment or cure for the benefit of future generations. A personal level of support and encouragement was given to the family at all times by the ataxia clinic at the National Hospital, and by Dr Paola Giunti in particular, whose genuine concern for Jane and willingness to help night and day went far beyond the call of duty. At all times, the message from the Ataxia Centre was positive. There was always something else that could be done, and this helped both of us to remain positive through the various hardships.

When we met at university, Jane was a staunch and vocal atheist. She remained a non-believer for most of her life. In 2011 things changed. Jane became seriously unwell and was placed under palliative care from home, with a prognosis of weeks to live. I was given the end-of-life talk. I was afraid we might lose her soon. Then, out of the blue, a true miracle happened. Jane, the girl who had sworn blind all her life that she would have nothing to do with religion, came dramatically to faith. Jane had (she told me later) been crying out to God for some time from her sickbed. When she told me this, I was puzzled and asked why she had cried out to God if she didn't believe He was there! It became apparent Jane's "atheism" was – and had always been – a mask for the pain of her dreadfully hard life. She told me that on that day Jesus Himself had come to her bedside and spoken to her. I asked her what Jesus had said, and Jane told me that He had placed His hand on her head and said, "Trust in Me!"

Amazed by this miracle, I led Jane to the verse in the Gospel of John where Jesus says, "Do not let your hearts be troubled. You believe in God; *trust also in me*" (John 14:1 NIV, emphasis added).

I asked Jane how she had replied to Jesus, and she told me she had placed her trust in Him immediately to save her and to take away her sin. She did not swerve from this decision to follow Christ. From an entrenched position where she would refuse to go anywhere near a church, and would become terribly angry whenever I mentioned the name of Jesus, Jane changed. She softened. Jane told me, that very day, that she wanted to start coming to church with me; that she wanted to visit Israel, to see the land where Jesus had lived and walked in the flesh; and that she wanted to be baptised. Jane and I were blessed with five more years together.

Before becoming a Christian in 2011, Jane got her strength from being in control, at all costs, of her feelings and her environment. When she came to faith, something changed. The change was subtle but profound. Jane's physical frailty remained evident to all, but the lifelong root of bitterness and anger towards God had gone. In her calmness and serenity, God's "strength was made perfect in weakness" (2 Corinthians 12:9 KJV). Right to the end of her life, Jane would be famous above all for her beautiful smile.

At last, Jane could be comforted. She explained to me that the anger, deep down, had been towards God, whom she had blamed for her condition, even though for decades she had insisted He did not exist. Now, Jane would weep buckets at the drop of a hat. Tears of joy. It was wonderful to be able to comfort her at last. It was as if she had at long last been set free to be herself. The mask had gone (and with it the friction of a life of pain).

In a very real sense, Jane was at last genuinely strong: no longer with an artificial strength based on brute denial of her condition and control of her environment, but rather with a deeper strength based on facing the truth. Jane was now ready to start writing her memoirs. It was clear to me this strength came from her faith in Christ. For Jane, the sentence "I can do all things through Christ who strengthens me" (Philippians 4:13 NKJV) was more than hollow sentiment or a religious edict. The promise was real and filled her with lasting hope in the darkest of days.

Those who hope in the Lord will renew their strength.
They will soar on wings like eagles;
They will run and not grow weary;
They will walk and not be faint.

Isaiah 40:29–31 NIV

Jane recovered from the worrying episode in palliative care, but from then on she found it noticeably harder to speak. The local neurological rehabilitation team based at the Memorial Hospital in Woolwich became involved and soon helped turn things around. They were led by the wonderful Adrian, the motorcycling "Matron", who looked more like a rugby forward than Hattie Jacques. Jane was seen regularly by speech therapists, occupational therapists, physiotherapists, dieticians, podiatrists, district nurses, and others. A new team of specialist carers were sent from a nursing agency. Without their dedicated and professional support, I would have had to give up work in 2011.

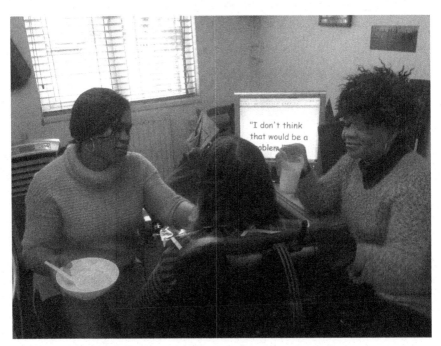

Jane with Emma and Theresa from the nursing agency

It was through the speech therapists that Jane's swallowing difficulty was first identified. She was offered a PEG feeding tube, to avoid choking, but she was terrified of the very idea of this and refused point-blank. Instead, to respect her wishes, we were shown how to blend interesting meals for her without lumps, and how to thicken her drinks sufficiently to limit the risk of aspiration without affecting the taste.

The speech therapy team were amazed that Jane had only just come to their attention. Her neurological condition was so advanced. They saw her needs as urgent. Through their insistence, Jane eventually received the assistive technology she would use to write *Forever Yours*. Jane was very grateful for this. She cared deeply that those who make decisions about priorities in the health-care system must realise how essential such equipment is and how important it is to give the most vulnerable in society (like herself) a chance to continue to communicate and be involved. It is no exaggeration to say that the assistive technology Jane received following her spell in palliative care changed her life dramatically and gave her real hope for the final five years of her life, the period during which *Forever Yours* was conceived and produced. Being able to communicate again at last, after so many years, meant everything to her.

So it was that in the midst of losing her voice, her hearing, and the use of her arms and her hands, Jane decided to write her autobiography, with her chin, using a special device attached to her wheelchair. She was to call her book *Forever Yours*. This was the inscription we had chosen for both of our engagement rings back in 1977. Jane told me her book was to be a love story, but with a twist. She planned to write of how we had found love all those years ago as students in Scotland and of how in middle age and against all odds she of all people had come to know the love of God in the person of Jesus Christ.

Jane could, up until mid to late 2013, still speak to me fairly normally, and I could mostly understand her (though with increasing difficulty). Between 2011 and 2014, Jane managed to produce the first part of *Forever Yours*, Chapters 1 to 20, up to the birth of Johnny in 1980. Around late 2014, Jane began to lose her speaking voice to a previously unknown and distressing extent. I now found it virtually impossible to understand her. The deterioration was rapid. At the same time her hearing deteriorated sharply, until she lost the ability to discern the speech of others, even in a quiet room. From then on, with regret and out of necessity, Jane stopped writing the formal chapters of the book and chose to write to me (and to others) instead.

For Jane, this decision must have been a tough one to make, but she gave the impression she still really loved writing, as at last she could be understood. Her style was succinct, partly through personal choice, but largely perhaps because in her case the writing process itself was so intensely difficult that she did not waste time with anything superfluous. Where Jane is concerned, every word counts. Her updates, newsletters, and wide-ranging remarks reveal another side of Jane: the person behind the book. They reveal who she was, what made her so special, and why she inspired (and continues to inspire) such love and admiration from all she ever met.

Now unable to chat with others, read the newspapers, browse the Internet, watch TV, or listen to the radio, Jane would write to me often to ask me to explain to her on screen what on earth was going on, both in the family and in the wider world. Jane and I now had our own private world: an on-screen world. Jane became increasingly detached towards the end from the world of sound and vision around her. She felt cut off, increasingly locked in but nevertheless desperate to understand and be understood. Jane used her Tobii almost exclusively to "talk" to me, painstakingly, night and day, instead of trying to vocalise speech and in lieu of completing the book (as planned) in its original format.

Progressively losing speech and hearing was, for Jane, the most distressing symptom of all. She would get upset often. It concerned her greatly that others could have no real conception of why she was unable to join in. She worried they might conclude she was slow or somehow lacking comprehension. We both knew that Jane's problems with hearing and speech were motor/sensory, rather than cognitive, as we could communicate in depth (albeit slowly) on screen, but this was hard to explain to others, including doctors. Jane would complain to me that as she grew older life seemed to just go on around her. She came to see herself as a spectator – later, perhaps even as an onlooker from afar. As the process of deterioration continued, it became harder for Jane to bury her emotions. At the point where denial no longer worked as an effective defence mechanism to keep her strong, she cried out to God and He answered. Together, and in faith, we were to learn that the deepest joy can come from the darkest of places, including in times of trial and pain.

Jane continued to write a sentence here, a sentence there, whenever she could manage during the period from 2014 to early 2016. For the past twenty years or more, I had been glad to act as interpreter on a daily basis. I could no longer help her with this. Having normal conversations as before became virtually impossible. It broke my heart to admit it, but now I too could barely understand a word Jane said.

Once a year, our doctor would send one of his young medical student trainees to visit our home as a learning exercise (part of their university course) to see how we coped as a family with the day-to-day realities of such a dreadful illness impacting every possible aspect of our lives. One particular student was moved by our situation and how we faced up to life's struggles. She said she was amazed by Jane's testimony and delighted that we both knew Jesus. She shared with us her favourite passage from Hebrews:

Our Compassionate High Priest

Seeing then that we have a great High Priest who has passed through the heavens, Jesus the Son of God, let us hold fast our confession. For we do not have a High

Priest who cannot sympathize with our weaknesses, but was in all points tempted as we are, yet without sin. Let us therefore come boldly to the throne of grace, that we may obtain mercy and find grace to help in time of need. (Hebrews 4:14–16 NKJV)

Such visits meant a great deal to Jane (coming from a medical family), as she felt she might in her own way have made a difference, however slight, in helping the next generation of doctors to understand the devastating reality of such little-understood genetic illnesses as Friedreich's ataxia. More importantly, Jane was living proof that no diagnosis is a death sentence. There is always light at the end of the tunnel. Giving in is not an option; giving up, still less so. Life is precious and every moment to be savoured.

In the 1990s we lived in Lee Green. One of Jane's home helps at the time was Jan, whom Jane had rated very highly. Jane thought Jan ought really to train as a nurse, because in her view Jan was cut out for nursing. Twenty-three years later, in 2015, Jane and I were to bump into Jan one day in Marks and Spencer, when we were out shopping. We had not seen Jan at all in the intervening years, as we had moved back to Eltham. Jan was keen to tell Jane that she had indeed taken her advice, many years ago, and had gone on to train as a nurse. She asked how Jane had managed to keep her skin still looking so good after so many years! Then she told Jane she now worked as a district nurse in Kent and loved her job – and it was all thanks to Jane's advice all those years ago. It thrilled Jane to hear this wonderful news after so many years.

As Jane's hearing deteriorated, we learned to improvise on the hoof. When friends came to see Jane, we would ask them to write down what they wanted to say to her on a large whiteboard, as this was so much easier for her to understand. At church, our friends, including Christine,

Guy, and Betty, would take turns using Jane's whiteboard to transcribe for her in large letters the gist of the sermon, as she could hear the speaker but no longer make out the words. Jane loved her whiteboard – the ultimate low-tech solution to complex hearing problems that are not remedied by amplification.

Towards the end of her life, Jane would chide me at times for still speaking to her out of habit (rather than writing on screen), as vocalised speech (even my voice) had by now become very hard for her to understand. She continued to smile and nod in company with others, but she would tell me afterwards she had no idea what people were saying. This was a bitter pill to swallow – one of many. Nevertheless, the desire to get her point across never left Jane. During 2014, Jane started to hear all the words she had struggled to say all day, spoken by others, in her mind, though she was fully aware they were not there in reality. She reported this symptom to her audiologist. Latterly, during 2015–2016, we would sit together side by side for hours on end, still struggling to communicate. On good days we would make progress slowly, one word at a time. At times it was like pulling teeth, but with pliers, and without the benefit of anaesthetic. This process was intensely painful for us both, but just being together meant everything to us. We had always been close, but now we were closer than ever. Jane found it harder and harder to write, until early 2016, when she finally lost the ability to use the Tobii. First, productivity reduced to a crawl, then to a word or two a day, next perhaps a letter or two, and finally to nothing at all. Silence.

On 29 February 2016, Jane took a turn for the worse and was admitted to our local hospital, the Queen Elizabeth in Woolwich. I wrote as follows to Jane's amazingly helpful and attentive consultant, Dr Giunti. She and her team at the Ataxia Clinic had been in close contact with us at the end of a telephone line each step of the way, for many years supporting the family. She clearly loved Jane and had done everything in her power to make Jane's life worth living, with much success along the way.

Dr Giunti,

This is to update you on Jane's condition since we last spoke.

The medicine you prescribed for Jane last year has given her a quality of life for the past few months that is so much more than I could have dared hope for back in September 2015. Thank you so much. She has until recently been calm and contented most of the time. She has been eating and drinking very well, and sleeping through the night with far less crying and screaming. We had a lovely Christmas with our son at home, and Jane was able to enjoy and to take part in all the festivities, including the food and drink, which she loved. She has been able on one or two occasions to come with me on the bus to the local Italian restaurant, for family meals with her 88-year-old father, which she also loved. Her last such meal was on Valentine's Day 2016 when she finished with a Bailey's milkshake. Atypical to the end. I made a little film for Jane to celebrate Valentine's Day 2016. She loved it.

Sadly, Jane is now in hospital again, with another chest infection. She had obstinately refused food or drink for over twenty-four hours (for reasons related to her end-of-life confusion), and not just once, but this is something that had been happening most weeks intermittently for some time now – and she was (once more) on the verge of a diabetic hypo, which as you know can cause coma and is very dangerous. Twice this week I had to gently administer glucose gel and fluids against her will, in order to keep her alive and raise her blood sugar to allow me to give her the insulin – with Jane struggling and screaming in protest, doing her utmost best to spit the Gluco-Gel back out. This is not something I could ever do again. *Harrowing* does not begin to do justice to the anguish of seeing Jane suffer like this, with no insight even into the reality of her need for insulin. In hospital she is on IV fluids, glucose, and antibiotics. She sleeps a great deal of the time. Medical people are in charge.

Jane's swallowing was assessed in hospital last week by the SALT team. They initially (quite correctly) recommended continuation of her long-standing and preferred pureed diet with thickened drinks. During the past week, however, Jane's swallowing, in my view, appears to have deteriorated further. I have told the nurses on the ward I now believe it is time to implement PEG feeding, as she has been choking so much more recently. Jane needed suction twice at mealtimes yesterday (Sunday) to clear her airways. We cannot continue like this.

Jane now needs one-on-one 24/7 nursing care. Her condition is so far advanced now that we simply can't cope at home. The repeated refusals to eat or drink – and the increase in choking when she does eat or drink – are truly overwhelming. With great reluctance I have to now concede that Jane needs residential nursing care 24/7.

Nothing arranged yet, but Jane, I'm afraid, will not this time be coming home from hospital. If she did, I myself would need a bed in hospital before the week was out. The words *last* and *straw* come to mind. Refusing to eat or drink (when she needs insulin) and choking (when she does eat or drink) were together the last straw.

My employers have been great and have given me some time off to visit Jane, so I can see her every day.

She is a happy little soul still. I took a photo today of her smiling, which will put your minds at rest. I've attached the photo here. Jane is very unwell and looks tired, but she is still happy much of the time. This is reassuring.

This is such a difficult time for us all, but we are coping as well as possible. Have a look at the attached photo of Jane. Prettier than ever.

Jane with Henry, February 2016

Thank you for all the love, help, and support you have shown us, beyond the call of duty, for so long and through such painful times. I will never forget your help and kindness to Jane. Our local health agencies, too, have been wonderfully supportive to us over the years and are there for us now more than ever. We have been blessed.

I am now hoping for a wonderful resolution to Jane's future needs (such as, ideally, local hospice care for Jane, where we can visit as often as possible, even after work). Jane deserves nothing but the best.

Jane went from hospital to a very nice local nursing home, where I was able to visit her every day after work. From her bed she had a lovely view overlooking the gardens. Jane enjoyed being fed small treats by mouth and having occasional sips of tea and juice. A few weeks later, however, she was very ill again and had to be returned to hospital. This time, in spite of excellent treatment from the medical staff, she did not improve. Jane died peacefully in her sleep in hospital on 4 May 2016, with her family by her side, and was taken home to Glory.

I've said enough. Time for Jane to speak …

The following poem was precious to Jane all her life. She recited this to me by heart in Bexleyheath in the summer of '77, soon after we got together. It always made her cry, but in a good way.

How Do I Love Thee? (Sonnet 43)
Elizabeth Barrett Browning, 1806–1861

How do I love thee? Let me count the ways.
I love thee to the depth and breadth and height
My soul can reach, when feeling out of sight
For the ends of being and ideal grace.
I love thee to the level of every day's
Most quiet need, by sun and candle-light.
I love thee freely, as men strive for right.
I love thee purely, as they turn from praise.
I love thee with the passion put to use
In my old griefs, and with my childhood's faith …
I love thee with the breath,
Smiles, tears, of all my life; and, if God choose,
I shall but love thee better after death.

Jane saw life as precious. She taught me, taught us all, the benefit, the necessity, of never giving up. Each word Jane herself produced in her last years is to be savoured like the finest wine; such was her struggle to produce them. I pray others will be moved by her words and by her story. And to Jane I say, as always, I love thee with the breath, smiles, tears, of all my life, and I remain *forever yours.*

Lightning Source UK Ltd.
Milton Keynes UK
UKOW01f0441070218
317466UK00002B/82/P

9 781973 611264